Made in New York

Made in New York

Handcrafted Works by Master Artisans

Nathalie and Ted Sann

Rizzoli
NEW YORK

New York Paris London Milan

First published in the United States of America in 2012
by Rizzoli International Publications, Inc.
300 Park Avenue South
New York, NY 10010
www.rizzoliusa.com

Foreword text © 2012 Jamie Drake

2012 2013 2014 2015 / 10 9 8 7 6 5 4 3 2 1

Design by Pentagram

Printed in China
ISBN: 978-0-8478-3801-1

Library of Congress Control Number: 2011938452

Contents

Foreword

Artisanship in New York is not only alive and well, it is thriving! As an aficionado of unique beauty, I was overcome with delight as I made my way through the pages of *Made in New York*. The Sanns' odyssey through the ateliers of such exceptional talent is a remarkable journey that they now share with lovers of handcrafted creations. The breadth, individuality, and variety of pursuits included within are truly epic. The range of materials featured is vast—metal, stone, wood, fabric, paper, plaster, glass, flowers, clay and much more—and the end results include pieces to wear, sit on, play with, look through, or walk upon. All are equally dazzling.

The practitioners in *Made in New York* pay homage to both the heritage of American arts and crafts, such as woodworking and metalsmithing, as well as those of European or Asian derivation, including glassblowing, stained glass, and decoupage. Their resulting creations are destined to become the heirlooms of our future generations.

The allure of the commissioned piece created specifically for a patron has been intoxicating and irresistible throughout history, from the Medicis of Renaissance Florence to the clients of Frank Lloyd Wright in the twentieth century. It is the vision of these commissioners, and the artisan creators, who have shaped cultural and aesthetic trajectories. The great landmarks of art, architecture, and design are the result of these ambitious collaborations.

The tradition of crafting items for personal and household use, fashioned with love, is of abiding importance today. We live in an era in which big box global chains dominate; in addition, online commerce, while groundbreaking in its convenience, threatens the livelihood of independent, local practitioners with each click of the mouse. The experience of visiting an atelier, smelling the materials, and imagining a commissioned work with the artist is quickly becoming a vestige of past generations. Thus, the legacy of handspun items of exquisite craftsmanship found herein is even more vital to the preservation of these arts and skills for the twenty-first century.

As an interior designer, I see this as a catalogue of creations that inspire dreams to emerge. To wear a chic fedora as I pass through foliate gates while walking on tiny mosaics, to knock on a marquetry door, then enter a foyer tinted with color from stained glass windows and scented with fresh cut flowers, while hearing the distant tinkling of piano keys—this is a fantasy still able to be realized right here in New York City.

As a New Yorker who has called this city my home for decades, I have huge home-grown pride in seeing these artisans. As a consumer I long to begin commissioning pieces from them for both my clients and myself. This book is a wonderful resource for the professional or the layperson alike. Beautifully illustrated and accessibly written, it is a necessary addition to the literature on artisanal practice and provides an opportunity to envision a future where quality and craftsmanship are paramount, where tradition can fuse with the contemporary, and where the relationship between the artisan and the consumer is still personal.

—Jamie Drake

Introduction

The idea for this book came out of a conversation with Renaud Dutreil, formerly minister of small business and craftsmanship in France and now chairman of LVMH North America—a group famously known for its culture of craftsmanship. Dutreil spoke about his efforts to preserve and protect the ancient métiers and to ensure their survival through legislation and a strong apprentice system. The conversation created inspiration to find a way to bolster enthusiasm for small trades here in the United States. Nathalie understood from the beginning that the route to acceptance and support for artisans in the United States would not be legislation, but rather education. *Made in New York* is one small step in that direction.

Nathalie and I have always had a great interest in the work of artisans. I am an inveterate reader of the *Whole Earth Catalogue*, and taker-on of projects such as guitar building and boat making, with varying degrees of success. Nathalie is a practitioner of several of the métiers described in this book. A master embroiderer, she studied at Lesage studio in Paris. She is also a fine gilder, a trade she learned at the Elizabeth O'Neill Studio, and a world-class seamstress.

Our first collaboration was the restoration of a seventeenth-century house in Sagaponack, New York. We worked with a fine architect, David Scott Parker, who at the time specialized in renovating classic period houses for modern clients. Together we decided that we wanted to preserve as much of the character of the house as we could, making certain areas more livable without sacrificing its spirit. The house was pretty much falling down, and after extensive structural repair, the project was flooded with artisans, including window makers—all of the new windows had to be made by hand to match the old—hardware forgers, cabinetmakers, and fireplace builders who worked with eighteenth-century brick. As we watched these craftsmen work, we were impressed not only by their skill, but also by their dedication. They weren't just showing up for work, they were joyously practicing their métiers.

This dedication and joy jumped out at us as we began to interview and photograph the artisans for this book. We were lucky enough to meet an exuberant neon sign maker (page 142), who gave up organic farming to pursue her craft, and a tiny glassblower (page 86) with all the energy of one of her fiery furnaces.

Their drive and passion made us think of all the people out there commuting to jobs they don't necessarily enjoy, who—had they been trained differently in a society that both respected and protected artisans—might be running to work instead of trudging. And of those whose jobs have moved offshore. We met one artisan, a true master, who had given up the old ways of working and was plying his craft in a completely mechanized studio. The work was uninteresting and dull, and the proprietor complained that most of his clients had turned to China as a supplier. He was unaware that by mechanizing his operation, he had turned his work into a commodity, and for commodities, all work goes to the lowest-cost producer.

But for artisans, the work is where they are: their skills, the uniqueness of their designs, and the quality of the work can't be duplicated elsewhere. One could not imagine sending a Tiffany window to China for restoration.

In France, the government has put in place an extensive program that includes a revamping of the apprentice system through schools such as École Boulle and the Atelier de Sèvres. As a result, the younger generation, among whom unemployment rates are soaring, is becoming more and more interested in learning the old crafts. The program has also provided a new respect for these craftspeople, giving them an honorable place in society.

In his book, *Shop Class as Soulcraft*, Matthew Crawford makes a strong argument for bringing manual-trades training back into the American secondary school curriculum. He believes that these are the trades that can't be exported, trades that put meaning into lives and get workers off the treadmill to nowhere. Crawford, an MIT graduate, worked for several years at a Washington, D.C., think tank, and finally quit to open a motorcycle repair shop. He said he was happier than he'd ever been; he made about the same salary and did far more thinking in the motorcycle shop than he ever did at the think tank.

We happily dedicate these pages to all the beautiful, passionate, and truly talented artisans we met in the course of putting together this book. Every last one of them was a joy to meet and to watch at their work. They welcomed us into their bustling studios with warmth and grace, often taking hours out of very busy schedules.

We hope this book will begin to change your perspective on artisans and artisanship in the United States, and in some small way demonstrate the artisans' value to our society, economically and socially. Most of all, we hope you will get out there and visit the artisans in this book, see how they work, and see the incredible work they turn out. We hope the experience will be as life changing for you as was for us.

Great thanks to Paula Scher who designed this book, Christopher Steighner who edited the book, Gaspar Dietrich who worked miracles on the photos in the lightroom, and Zoe G. Settle who gave much needed help on the text.

—Nathalie and Ted Sann

**Architectural
Hardware
Maker**

E. R. Butler & Co.
55 Prince Street
New York, NY 10012
212 925 3565
www.erbutler.com

Rhett Butler is a young entrepreneur with a vision of striking the perfect balance between craftsmanship, history, and technology. His company, E. R. Butler, may only date to 1990, but the history of beautiful, not just functional, hardware dates back centuries. His showroom at 55 Prince Street in Manhattan's SoHo neighborhood was, until 1897, the home of Prince Street Works, the silver department of Tiffany & Co. Today, Butler designs and produces custom architectural and cabinetry hardware such as bolts, escutcheons, knobs, levers, locks, pulls, and more, with a focus on American styles including Federal and Georgian.

Butler seeks out old, established companies, such as the Italian firm G. Bonomi & Figli and Boston's Vaughan, and approaches them about translating their hardware to the modern day without compromising style or quality. He obtains their catalogues and molds, and then reinvents them with his own twist. A cornerstone of his modern-day approach is his direct outreach to others, such as jewelry designer Ted Muehling, asking them to collaborate and translate their work to the medium of hardware. Butler's candlesticks, a bit of a departure from the core business, are among the company's most recognizable products.

The Butler showroom, open only to members of the interior-design trade, is where the designers modify and bring historic hardware to the next level, creating period hardware with the attributes and aesthetics of the present day. The designers draw or remodel much of the hardware in 3-D on a computer. While still incorporating handcrafted techniques, they trust the technology to make the pieces as efficiently as possible with the highest-quality materials.

Since 1997, part of Butler's production has been done in a factory in Red Hook, Brooklyn, in a spectacular redbrick building the company has been renovating little by little. This is where the hardware is cast and finished. One room is filled with the latest high-tech machinery; next door is a finishing room where one artisan hand-polishes a Ted Muehling doorknob to just the right patina while another gilts a gold-leaf knob. Although functional hardware is easy to come by, Butler has cultivated a following for his aesthetically beautiful creations, successfully elevating hardware to an art form.

**Art
Conservator**

Simon Parkes
02 East 74th Street
New York, NY 10021
12 734 3920

In New York City, art is big business, and the preservation and conservation of art is a significant enterprise in its own right. The Institute of Fine Arts at New York University offers a doctorate in art preservation, a degree that requires proficiency in art history, organic chemistry, painting, and German and Latin, and takes more than six years to complete. So it is highly unusual that the most respected conservator of oil paintings in the city is Simon Parkes, a man without any formal academic training.

Born in the United Kingdom, Parkes left school at age seventeen to work for an art conservator in London. Now, nearly forty years later, his New York atelier is the destination of choice for top auction houses, collectors, and galleries around the world. He can handle just about any work of art with a checkered past, from a Picasso that has spent years on the walls of a houseful of smokers to a blistered and cracked Vasari that was left out in the rain at an airport cargo facility.

Parkes's studio takes up two floors in what was a nineteenth-century carriage house, half a block from the East River on Manhattan's Upper East Side. On the first floor, one conservator sets up an ingenious heat-and-suction contraption to remove a potentially damaging wax backing from a still-life painting valued at several hundred thousand dollars. One misstep and the work will be ruined—but the conservator brims with confidence and smiles. Upstairs in the well-lit painting studio, in front of large, north-facing windows, another restorer removes tiny imperfections and cracks on a sixteenth-century Flemish painting on oak. She uses special paints that can be easily removed, if necessary. Parkes and most modern conservators believe restoration should be minimally invasive. This, however, was not always the widely held belief in conservation; in the past, restorers used a much heavier hand, so a considerable amount of Parkes's time is spent undoing the work of his overzealous predecessors.

**Basket
Weaver**

nathan Kline
26 Mott Evans Road
umansburg, NY 14886
7 387 5718
ww.blackashbaskets.com

Basket making is an age-old craft, a tradition, and it was still thriving in the Hudson Valley when Jonathan Kline grew up there in the 1960s. He spent hours watching artisans in the Shaker and Taghkanic communities near his home, finally learning the craft himself in 1980 from Newt Washburn, a fourth-generation basket maker. He was mesmerized by the prospect of using minimal tools to create a functional, beautiful object from a native tree. While most baskets are fashioned from reed, Kline's are made from splint, which has a very different feel.

Kline lives in one of the last areas with plentiful stands of American Black Ash trees, which are noted for their ability to separate easily along their annular layers, a trait prized by Native American basket weavers. Estimates show that the species will be completely extinct in the next ten years, so Kline is trying to take stock of as many as possible. When he receives a new pile of trees, he leaves it to dry for six months to a year. Then, in one part of the studio, he cuts the logs lengthwise so that he can then peel off long, reedlike strips of wood that he pounds with steel and slices to the desired width before smoothing the edges.

The basic construction of each basket is quite similar: Kline starts by weaving a square or rectangular bottom, and from there any variation is possible. He soaks each splint before weaving it, and ties it in place to hold shape throughout the process. The weaving looks effortless but it requires tremendous patience, strength, and a sturdy hand. Some baskets are then painted, which in the past was also used as a way to extend the piece's life. Kline makes his own nontoxic paints with mineral pigments and applies a natural linseed oil topcoat. He sells his baskets around the country and on his website, and welcomes custom orders.

Bicycle
Builder

oast Cycles
0 Troutman Street
rooklyn, NY 11206
46 724 1596
ww.johnnycoast.com

The basic structure of a bike never changes, so there isn't much room for "reinventing the wheels"—only refining aesthetics and performance. A one-man show based in Bushwick, Brooklyn, Johnny Coast has been building custom bikes in his eponymous atelier for years. His dad taught him welding at a young age, and he honed his bike-making skills at the United Bicycle Institute. He then perfected the craft at the legendary Koichi Yamagushi bike shop. His timing luckily coincided with a sort of "bicycle renaissance," due in part to the rise of the green movement and the price of gas. With the resurgence of biking, makers have also rediscovered vintage models and developed new capabilities, generating real excitement among bike fanatics.

Bike makers around the world have created a close-knit online community so they can easily get and give advice, or just share war stories. This is especially important since most of them work alone. Coast's studio is set up in an old garage in the back of a house next door to a church. In fitting artistic nonchalance, the address doesn't match the entrance location; frustrated visitors sometimes find themselves driving around the block. Coast is shy but very friendly, and his studio seems like a perfect fit for a guy with beautiful bird tattoos sleeved on both arms.

Commissioning a bike from Coast involves an interview and measurement process to determine what sort of bike the customer would like, and for what purpose (racing, cruising). Then comes the fitting and, finally, the question of color.

The result is a bicycle of great beauty—hand-brazed from rare Reynolds steel tubing and finished with precision.

**Billiards
Maker**

latt Billiards
09 Broadway
ew York, NY 10003
12 674 8855
www.blattbilliards.com

In the early 1900s, there were more than 400 game rooms in New York City alone. In 1923, Sam Blatt started to make billiard tables to capitalize on the popularity of the game. At one point, three generations of Blatts worked side by side; then Sam passed his business on to his son, Maurice. Now located on six floors on Broadway, across from the Strand Book Store, the business is run by Maurice's son, Ron, and his son, Paul, and the focus has turned to the antique side of the business: selling and restoring tables, with an emphasis on completely custom, high-end, handmade tables and accessories for connoisseurs.

A pool table has set requirements for stability and playability, but the cosmetic options are limitless. A client picks the style (classic or contemporary) and the finishes (woods, stains, leather for the pockets) for the traditional body. For special orders, Paul starts with a rough drawing, and then sets the Computer-Aided Design artists to work. All of the pieces are crafted in various workshops on the premises, each on a different floor, so the old elevator is in constant motion as it moves parts between floors. On the top floor, artisans paint, tan leather, create complex marquetry, inlay, and turn wood to precisely match missing table legs. Most of the artisans have been here for years. Many are trained as cabinetmakers, and a great many come from the Steinway piano factory in Astoria. For the full year before retirement, a master artisan works with a younger artisan apprentice to train him or her in the craft so that it lives on.

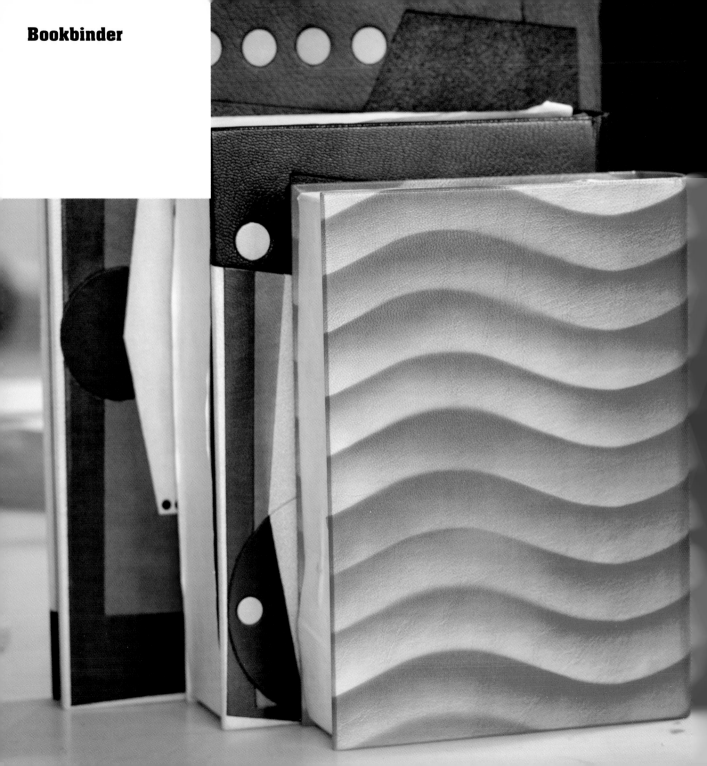

Bookbinder

Paper Dragon Books
80 Morgan Avenue, Suite 301
Brooklyn, NY 11211
718 782 8100
www.paperdragonbooks.com

Gavin Dovey learned the traditional art of bookbinding from Mark Cockram in the United Kingdom, which has a rich bookbinding history. Dovey moved to the United States and set up a studio in Brooklyn in 2005, with his wife and partner, Denise. Little by little, they began amassing the expensive tools and equipment, and now specialize in fine art and design binding.

Dragon Paper's bindings include bookbinding, case binding, box making, and presentation packaging. The work is very physical and also extremely precise. There are myriad skills involved: sewing by hand, cutting edges, sanding surfaces, hand-punching holes, working leather and understanding how it will react, cutting hides, gold-leafing, embossing, stamping, and building cases. The studio's bathroom is filled with dyes used for their craft. Sometimes these steps take weeks, but if an interesting project comes up at the last minute, the artisans will work around the clock to make it happen. While some clients provide detailed directions on projects, others simply send a book and trust the Doveys' creativity. Some clients they've never actually met, while others are repeat, frequent clients.

The Doveys love to translate this old-world practice into today's aesthetic sensibility. Recently, Gavin created a few leather hard cases for books, which he painted over with an airbrush, almost like graffiti. This freedom of self-expression is what he relishes about New York, compared with the craft he learned in England.

HUNTER S. THOMPSON

Calligrapher

Bernard Maisner
165 West 66th Street, Suite 8K
New York, NY 10023
212 477 6776
www.bernardmaisner.com

Even if you don't know his name, you've likely seen Maisner's work in the movies. He has arguably the most ornate, beautiful handwriting strokes around. He works from his home in Bay Head, New Jersey, in an atelier filled with paper, ink, drawing, pens, antique writing tools, books, and, of course, quills. The only sound here is his pen nib touching paper.

When Maisner was in high school, his father gave him a calligraphy set for his birthday. Soon thereafter, a passion and a business were born. Initially, he made creative lettering for advertising agencies, but computers nearly ate up his business with their ability to copy his cursive and adapt it as a font. Technology has been constantly evolving throughout his career, forcing Maisner to adjust and refine his path along the way. Now foe has become friend, and he has found ways to incorporate the computer into his work.

He sits at a table, warms up his long, beautiful hand, starts to draw, and then scans the work into a computer where he can perfect the letters and drawings. These days, one of his great challenges is not the emergence of new technology, but the disappearance of the old. Another one is the lack of suppliers for nibs: he prefers the classic ones, and the flexible nib of an old fountain pen. He mixes his own ink to achieve the right color, consistency, and tonality. The finished product then goes to his engraver who creates the envelope, invitation, stationery, or other printed material. Sometimes he works eighteen or nineteen hours a day, on an art he compares to playing an instrument—passing the moment where he no longer actively thinks about what he is doing, and just letting his hand move.

Carpenter

Miya Shoji
5 West 26th Street
New York, NY 10001
212 243 6774
www.miyashoji.com

Under the elevated train in Long Island City, Queens, on a street of one-story body shops and foundries, a steel door rolls up and reveals what looks like a diorama at the American Museum of Natural History: the pristine and timeless Japanese woodworking shop of Miya Shoji.

But the shop is no still life; all six carpenters work with great intensity in eerie, monastic silence. The front of the shop is built of concrete and cinder block, but in the back—where the master carpenter works on a raised platform—the floor, ceiling, and walls are sheathed in wood scraped smooth and clean once a week. Individual workstations are all variations on the traditional Japanese workbench, which is simply a very long, horizontal, four-by-four wood beam, mounted either on sawhorses or tables.

With a few minor exceptions, all the carpentry here is performed with traditional Japanese tools. The primary ones are pull saws that cut with scalpel-like precision, chisels of all sizes with lethally sharp edges, and beautifully crafted wooden planes that shave a uniform ribbon of wood with each stroke. Here, the artisans use sandpaper to flatten the tops of dowels; all smoothing is done with a formidable series of hand planes. In the hands of the master craftsman, Hakamata-san, these planes produce a silky, almost lacquerlike finish on raw wood.

The craftsmen primarily make *shoji* screens—sliding wooden mullion frames "glazed" with papers of varying lucidity—though they do make other original pieces of Japanese furniture. A *shoji* screen not only provides a way of dividing a space, but also suggests intrigue: Is something more interesting happening on the other side? Think of it as a bridge between a conventional wall, which completely blocks any adjoining space, and a wide opening that reveals everything next door. The *shoji* screen creates allure for the adjoining space, even though it might actually be less interesting than the current one. These screens can quickly turn an air-shaft view into a scintillating play of light and shadow. Miya's showroom is located in Manhattan on West 26th Street. Here, visitors can look over samples or help to design a *shoji* layout perfect for their space.

One last note on the traditions of this remarkable shop: every day at exactly noon, the workers break for lunch; at 12:30 p.m., they roll down the iron gate for an hour-and-a-half nap; and at 2:00, they roll up the door and the shop again begins to buzz quietly.

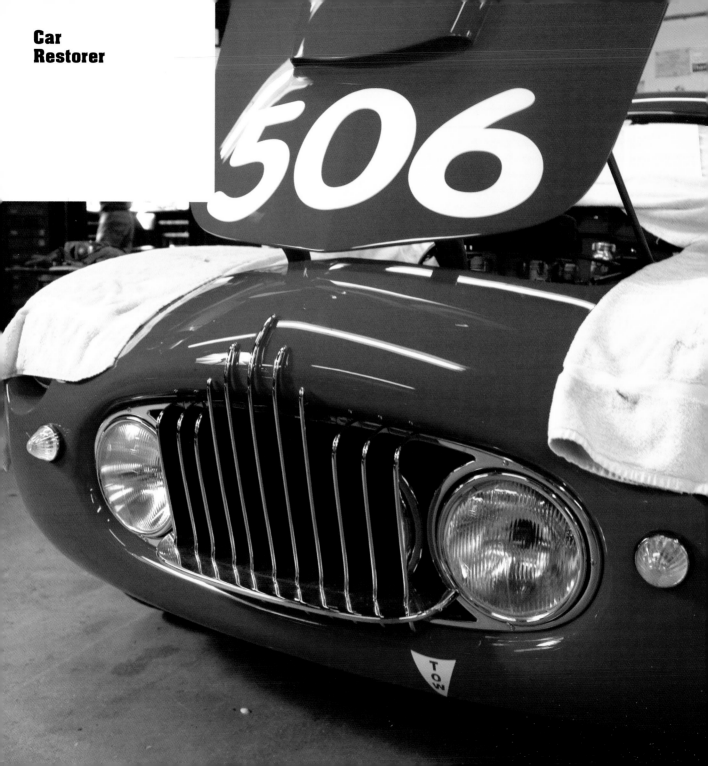

Northumberland Engineering
18 Mariner Drive
Southampton, NY 11968
1 287 2213
www.northumberlandenterprises.com

Let's face it: most Hamptons itineraries do not include an excursion to the local auto body shop. But Tony Dutton's atelier might just make beachgoers rethink their afternoon plans. Dutton and his team consider the cars they work on, not their owners, their customers; actually, their goal is to have the car survive its owner. His human clients seem equally committed to the conservation of the cars.

Dutton's family has been in the car industry in northern England since 1900. He's part Scottish, part English, and was raised in Northumberland where his father raced motorcycles. Dutton attended engineering college and worked on the local racetrack to earn money; he never raced himself because he was always more transfixed by the interior engineering of the machines.

Stepping into Dutton's atelier is almost like visiting a museum of rotating engines. Four mechanics work full time at the atelier, and it's not unusual for a former employee to return to work on a car that is his or her specialty or passion. There's also one retired team member who still comes in every day to see the latest project and enjoy a cup of coffee with old friends.

Tony knows how to build and fix a car, but his business mostly revolves around servicing cars. He credits his "sixth sense" for his successful track record—almost all of the cars that his team works on, including Aston Martins, Bentleys, and Ferraris, were built in very limited editions, so they all react differently.

Dutton travels all over the world to fix, maintain, and test cars. In France, for instance, he works on the Louis Vuitton collection. His experience, knowledge, and world travels have elevated his standing in the "car community"; he knows where to find critical pieces and how to go about building new ones. Sometimes his craft can be very expensive, but he believes that any work invested in a car will increase its longevity and value; luckily, his customers agree.

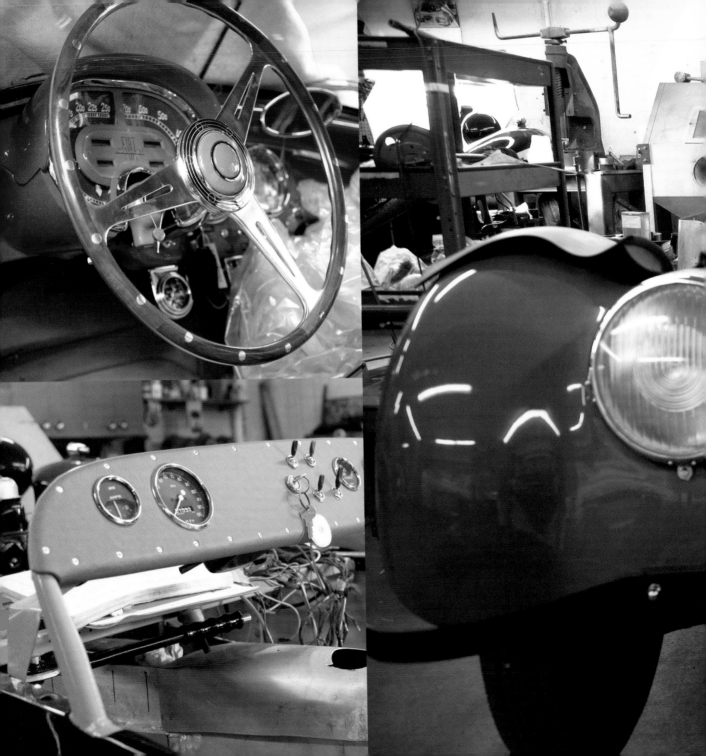

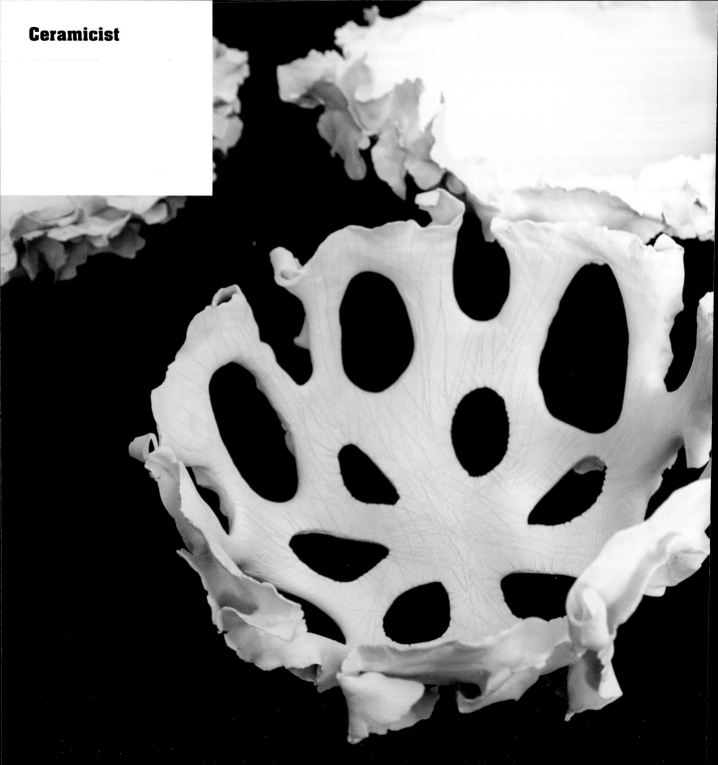

Inma Barrero
29 East 77th Street
New York, NY 10028
46 221 1814

When crafting a bowl or pot, Inma Barrero never thinks about how her ceramics will be used. She brings a Japanese mentality to her métier—there is no line between art and craft, utility and aesthetic. For as long as she can remember, she has been a creative person, in tune with her clay. Barrero studied ceramics in San Francisco, then moved to New York and joined a studio in Queens before starting her own studio in the back of the church where she lives. She continues to divide her time between her own studio and the one in Queens. She relishes the energy of being with other potters and learning from them.

For Barrero, clay is an intuitive medium, but at the same time a very technical material. She believes that it's not enough just to express oneself through the clay; one must also understand the medium, including its limitations when exposed to humidity and how a glaze changes during firing. Her craft is, on the one hand, pure and honest, and yet, on the other, highly complex. Clay is constantly evolving: whether wet or dry, it is rarely the same in its transparency, which can depend on the composition of the earth that surrounds it in the ground.

Barrero is inspired by nature. She uses traditional pottery tools and woodcarving implements; sometimes, she even relies on items from a kitchen supply store. Of course, her most utilized tools are her hands, which she believes reveal the feeling, movement, and expression contained within the clay—and are responsible for the beauty expressed in the final piece.

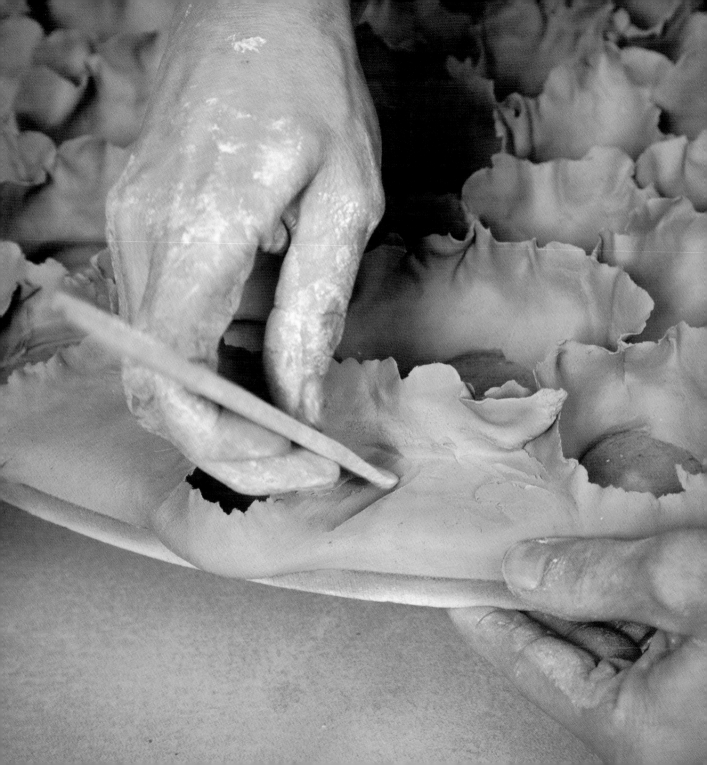

Decoupage
Artist

John Derian Company

East 2nd Street

ew York, NY 10003

2 677 3917

ww.johnderian.com

There's a beauty to John Derian—his height, soft voice, good manners—that seems to belong to a bygone era. Everything in his Manhattan decoupage shop is done by hand, including client and purchase orders, before they are entered into a computer. Derian, a Boston native, remembers making crafts his whole life. He started selling decoupage and faux-finished boxes to different stores in Boston before decamping to New York. He was happy just making boxes, until a store asked if he could do something on a plate for a client. That's when the orders started to pour in. Eventually, he opened a store on 2nd Street in Manhattan's East Village. Now he also owns another store next door and an atelier on the Bowery.

Derian starts all projects by brainstorming with his team for new patterns and browsing his collection of old imagery books and paper, which he continues to amass on his travels. He is also fascinated by nature and nineteenth-century organic and vegetable shapes. Derian uses a large printer to manipulate the scale of his inspiration, and then creates a composition of elements and a color template. Next, he brings this template downstairs to his store to see what it's best suited for: a box, lamp, paperweight, plate, or vase. Curved pieces are more challenging than flat ones.

The studio is very quiet, just like its owner. It resembles a large cabinet of curiosities: its walls are lined with Derian's collection, and its spaces are filled with the childhood smell of Elmer's Glue and the sound of scissors cutting paper. Artists are at work cutting shapes, drawing to prepare the positioning of the design, gluing the design with a brush and applying it to the back of the object, and removing excess glue with a sponge. Once a piece is finished, it is left on a simple kitchen rack to dry. Each work involves fifteen steps—from the beginning to the hand-signing on the back.

Decoy
Carver

Robert Hand
03 Madison Street
ag Harbor, NY 11963
31 725 2314

Duck decoys woven out of reeds, swamp grass, and duck feathers, recently unearthed in a Nevada cave, date to approximately A.D. 250, which makes this art form one of the oldest indigenous American crafts. Through the middle of the twentieth century, decoys were working tools, made to lure flocks of fowl to hunters. Today, many hunters still believe that the success of the hunt depends on the quality of the decoy.

Robert Hand Sr. is a decoy carver based in Sag Harbor, New York, who learned the craft from his father, an amateur carver, and took it up full time after serving in the Marines. His success was immediate: his Ruddy Duck won Best in Show at the 1978 U.S. National Decoy Carvers Show.

The skillful carving of a duck decoy is critical but almost as important is selecting the appropriate species of wood. Hand's shop brims with ricks of well-seasoned maple, tupelo, and other varieties. He prefers glued-up wood to a single block, for the control of proportion and grain direction, as well as the quality of the wood. Hand cuts several strips in the approximate size and weight of the live species and then glues and clamps them together. Next, he traces a precise paper pattern onto the four surfaces of the block. He uses an enormous band saw to create a rough shape before he starts to carve the decoy by hand. He works from picture books, taxidermy models, and memory, verifying the pattern every few minutes. Once he has completed the carving, he moves across to a curtained-off painting area. He calls himself a "brush freak," showing off hundreds of tiny, exquisite brushes of Kalinsky sable in ceramic cylinders. He coats the whole form in a single-color gesso before bringing the bird to life with other colors.

Some of Hand's decoys are show birds painted in minute detail; others are gunners, or hunters' working decoys. Even for the gunners, which don't require as much detail to fool a duck, he strives for painstaking accuracy, pushing himself, he says, "to go way past just fooling a bird." This is the sign of devotion to a craft, and why each of Hand's gunners takes at least seven weeks to complete; a show bird takes a few months.

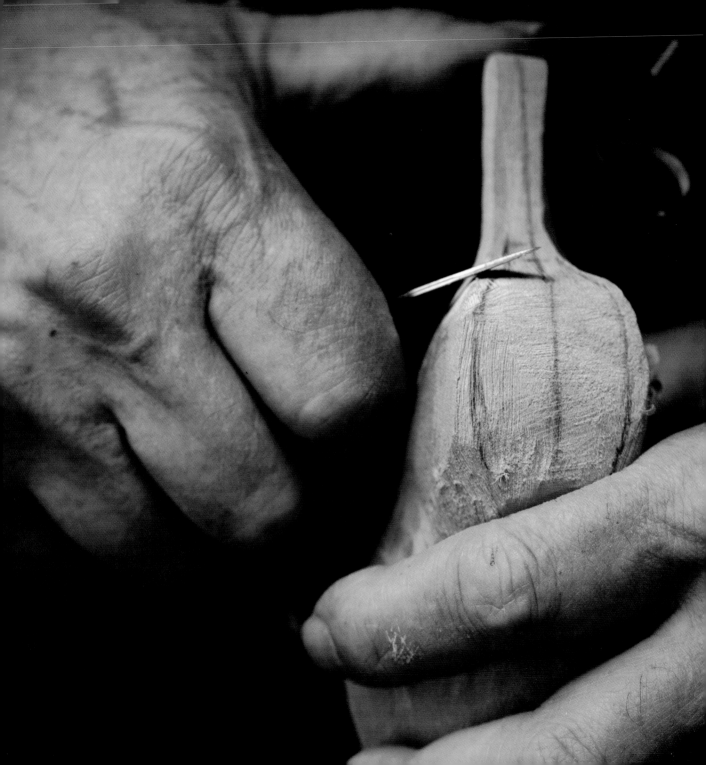

Embroiderer

enn & Fletcher
-07 41st Avenue, 5th Floor
ong Island City, NY 11101
2 239 6868
ww.pennandfletcher.com

The worlds of theater, fashion, interior design, and historical reproduction all rely on Penn & Fletcher's embroidery work. Started in 1986 as a lace and trim company by Andrew B. Marlay and Ernest A. Smith, Penn & Fletcher snapped up the talented workers from an industry that hadn't had much work since the 1950s, when embroidery work began to be contracted to overseas factories. The space now houses fifteen artists, a handful of cats for company, and two hundred embroidery machines from the 1800s. A showroom next to the warehouse highlights the workers' ability to realize anything with a textile and a stitch, both hand- and machine-embroidered air tucking, appliqué, Beauvais, braiding, chain stitching, chenille, crewel, edge pinking, quilting, ruffling, smocking, stump work, trapunto, and so on.

The company's on-site library contains thousands of patterns. An oversized computer, its sophisticated software, and its operator enable workers to sew intricate patterns in any scale limited only by the machine's memory. But its memory is forgiven, for the scale it can achieve is what distinguishes the company from any other embroidery house. Another station includes a stamping room with ultraviolet light and an antique perforating machine that separates delicate fabrics.

Working with old mechanical devices is challenging, not only because of their inevitable lack of precision, but especially because they often need to be repaired. Soft-spoken co-owner Ernie, with his penetrating blue eyes, is always donning a leather apron, and has scissors and a tape measure at the ready. He compares the repairs to fixing old cars, which he does as a hobby. Miraculously, he's always been able to find a needed part so that business can continue as usual.

Floral Designer

'Olivier Floral Atelier
9 East 76th Street
ew York, NY 10021
12 774 7676
13 West 14th Street
ew York, NY 10011
12 255 2828
ww.lolivier.com

Olivier Giugni arrived in New York City twenty years ago, and after a one-year stint at a local flower shop learning how to cut flowers, he was ready for his next endeavor. Armed with the job listings section of a French newspaper, he found the legendary restaurant Maxim's was looking for a florist. Pierre Cardin himself, a fixture in the fashion, design, and restaurant world, and a true flower lover, interviewed him. The two collaborated beautifully, with the flower shop next door to the restaurant. It was Cardin, with his fashion background, who thought to have foliage wrap the floral arrangement. (He hated bringing beautiful flowers to friends only to have them go to waste because no one knew what to do with them; he believed that they should be presented in a beautiful vase appropriate for the arrangement.)

Olivier immediately invented a new technique of wrapping leaves around flowers, mimicking a dress. This also solved the problem of how to adjust the arrangement when water needed to be changed in the vase: he simply used another leaf wrap inside the vase. None of this seems particularly notable these days, but at the time it was a totally novel concept.

Today, Olivier has two storefronts, thirty employees, and a division dedicated to special events, and yet the process is still the same. Every day at five o'clock in the morning, one employee visits the 28th Street Flower Market to buy fresh flowers. (Olivier also buys flowers directly from nurseries in France and Holland, depending on seasonal availability.) Meanwhile, others are at work on arrangements for hotels and restaurants; they also refresh arrangements on site during the week. For a while when he first started out, Olivier also terraced landscapes for clients. While he no longer officially provides this service, he will sharpen his pruning shears if a dear client makes a special request.

Floral design is an art form that requires minimal tools—a good pair of scissors and a sharp knife—and ultimately, all one really needs is a sense of the flower and of design. Olivier's employees have cultivated these skills over time; many of them have worked at the 14th Street studio for years. Olivier provides them with direction but trusts them completely. As he says, "In the morning, I like to have a happy client, happy employees, and, if there is a little bit more than that, I will take it."

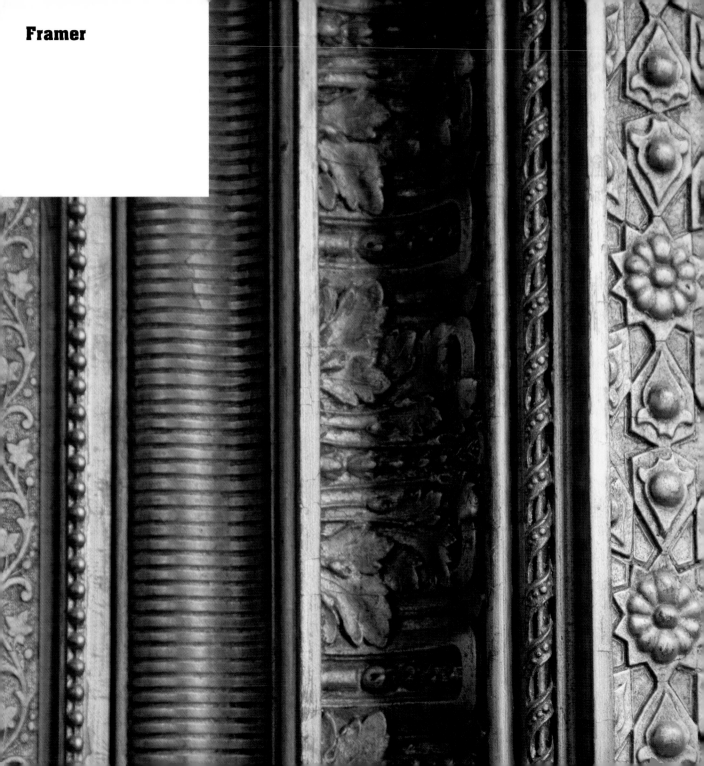

Framer

Eli Wilner & Company
1525 York Avenue
New York, NY 10028
212 744 6521
www.eliwilner.com

Trained as a painter, Eli Wilner learned at a young age that good art needs a good frame. His great-aunt and great-uncle first opened his eyes to art. At age nine, his great-uncle hooked him when he framed one of the young boy's own paintings. Wilner started his own business at age twenty-seven, translating skills he learned building sailboats into crafting beautiful frames. He now works out of a Manhattan town house on York Avenue, which is filled with both antique and contemporary frames, each labeled with a name, date, and price. Wilner and his team also reproduce and restore antique frames.

When he first started the business, frames were not their own industry. He was a pioneer in the field, spending much time antiquing and then refurbishing and selling frames. He's since established a following of museums, including the Metropolitan Museum of Art, which has relied on his skills since 1990. Nowadays, it's not unusual for an auction house to borrow more than 700 of his frames at a time. This means that Wilner and his team regularly travel the world for clients and their collections. Wilner even visited the White House to present a lecture, which resulted in a commission for twenty-eight of his frames.

Wilner, who is essentially the company's creative director, personally reviews every frame that his artisans produce. Even as the business expands—Wilner now has an atelier in Long Island City, Queens—he knows all of his employees, many of whom have worked for him for more than twenty years. Wilner's Manhattan showroom, where all of the marketing and designing is done, looks like a museum. The Long Island City location houses the company's workshops and serves as a storage facility for frames of all periods and sizes. At work are wood carvers, casters, and gilders, each toiling at his or her own station but with a great deal of collaboration.

Every new frame is designed digitally before any work begins. Wilner's team can make frames in any size. All of the base woods are indigenous to the United States, although the final products wind up in homes and museums as far away as China. For two years, the company has been at work on the renovation of the frame for Emanuel Gottlieb Leutze's famous 1851 painting, *Washington Crossing the Delaware.*

Furniture Conservator

Fine Wood Conservation, Ltd.
31 Van Brunt Street
Brooklyn, NY 11231
718 802 1659
www.woodconservation.com

Walk into Olaf Unsoeld and Cornelis van Horne's expansive studio on the long wharf in Red Hook, Brooklyn, and you are in the storehouse of treasures from the Indiana Jones movie, *Raiders of the Lost Ark*. Except here you will find magnificent examples of period furniture ranging from the Middle Ages to the twenty-first century: an ornately carved and gilded satinwood 1906 Chickering grand piano, severely damaged by Hurricane Katrina; a Louis Majorelle armoire; and a Donald Judd desk. From Biedermeier to Jugendstil, pieces arrive at the studio to be carefully treated to preserve original materials and surfaces, or, if needed, sensitively repaired or restored.

Unsoeld and Van Horne started the company in 1990 in Philadelphia, and relocated in 1994 to Brooklyn, where they do museum-quality work. Rather than advertise, they rely on word of mouth among clients, and as a result have become the gold standard for wood conservation. They have undertaken projects for world-renowned museums, including the Neue Galerie in New York, the Art Institute of Chicago, the Wolfsonian Museum in Miami Beach, the Judd Foundation, the Metropolitan Museum of Art, the Cooper-Hewitt Museum, and the Brooklyn Museum.

At the workbenches between the columns and along the stone walls of the waterfront Civil War–era warehouse, the small group of master craftsmen inset veneer, repair broken joinery, and carve missing elements. Original gilding is gingerly exposed or re-gilded if missing, and original finishes uncovered or re-created if previously lost or damaged.

The patina of an old piece is precious, and Unsoeld and Van Horne make every effort to preserve it. To discern the maker's intent, they go as deeply into the history of a piece as they can. Together, they decide just how much work can be done on a piece before its original essence disappears beneath all the repair and restoration. Unsoeld and Van Horne are very careful to take a project only as far as their finely tuned aesthetic will allow, using restoration materials contemporary with each piece that won't interfere with future restorations. Unsoeld holds a graduate degree from the Yale School of Forestry and Environmental Studies, and he believes that every time he preserves an old wood piece he saves at least a portion of a hardwood tree from destruction. Another unique feature of the studio is a fully realized apprentice program that allows students from all over the world to work under the tutelage of the masters for up to six months.

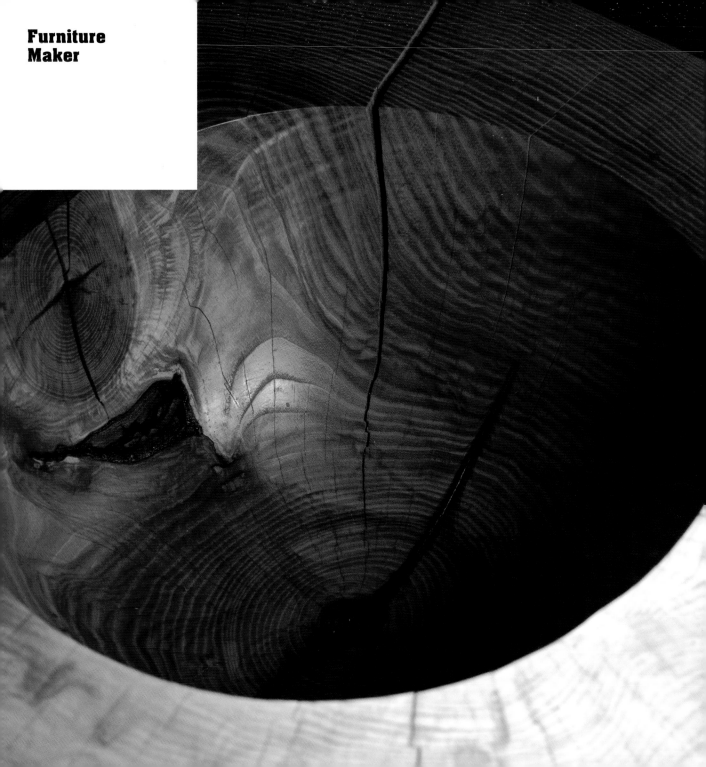

hris Lehrecke
5 Warren Street
udson, NY 12534
45 802 6187
ww.chrislehrecke.com

Approaching the studio of Chris Lehrecke in upstate New York, enormous piles of wood—all from local sources—reveal his craft. The furniture maker lives in a former church on a beautiful piece of property with his wife, Gabriella Kiss, a jewelry designer. A barn on the land serves as his studio, whose first floor is filled with all sorts of equipment, both new and old. He's been collecting cutting tools, machinery, and materials for more than twenty years. It looks like a beautiful showroom with works in progress scattered among finished pieces.

With a background in graphic design, Lehrecke learned furniture making from a designer in Brooklyn. In the 1980s, he joined a group of emerging artists in New York, although his work stood out because it was not as provocative as the rest. Today, he prides himself on the craftsmanship and individuality of each piece. His designs straddle the line between organic and restrained, with some pieces referencing the American Arts and Crafts movement and the work of architect Frank Lloyd Wright. Lehrecke is particularly inspired by Shaker styles and sometimes plays with a touch of mid-century Danish design, although he also cites the aesthetic styles of African and Japanese cultures as influences. Ultimately, he creates timeless furniture for collectors who want to invest in designs for the next generation.

Lehrecke works primarily with cherry, maple, and walnut, all native American species. The wood must first dry thoroughly; during this time, cracks are naturally created. He may then spend hours sanding a single piece of wood with increasingly finer grits until it feels like silk. Next, he oils and varnishes the wood in several coats. He believes wood should be oiled as much as possible to keep it looking alive, as though it were in its natural state. His work is prominently seen at the farm-restaurant Blue Hill at Stone Barns, and while he continues to design collections for Ralph Pucci (see page 128), where he's been represented for years, he now mostly creates custom pieces for individuals.

Glassblower

Michiko Sakano Glass
232 3rd Street, Suite E001
Brooklyn, NY 11215
917 783 0893
www.michikosakano.com

Michiko Sakano might be trained in the traditional Venetian style of glassblowing, but her affinity for bright color definitely comes from growing up in the 1970s. She is incredibly humble, and tells clients that the real artist in her family is her mother, a renowned kimono maker who lives in Kanazawa, Japan.

Sakano grew up straddling Japanese and American identities and cultures. These days, she divides her time between two studios in Brooklyn: one at One Sixty Glass, where she blows the glass, and the other at the Can Factory, where she fabricates and finishes the pieces. One Sixty Glass is a large facility where visitors can buy glassware, take a class, or rent a studio. Opening the door to the studio is like embarking on a field trip to Murano, Italy, complete with a sprawling panorama of glass and workers.

Sakano is experimental, welcoming collaborations with other glass artists such as Lindsay Adelman (on lamp parts) and adding different materials, including gold leaf that she blows into the glass to create new effects. She works silently and deliberately with her assistant, and no matter the season, it's hot in the studio. First, she warms the glass on a heavy blowing pipe until it becomes very soft and malleable. Then, she begins to blow the glass. The extremely high temperatures are necessary to shape the glass but she must be careful—it can become liquid, at which point it is unworkable. Yet glass can't be shaped until it is heated to a soft consistency.

Either she or her assistant sits on the bench, blowing, while the other shapes the piece using tongs and places it over the heat until the desired shape is achieved. Then the glass is cut from the blowing pipe with specially designed scissors and left to cool. Nowadays, much glass is industrially produced, without imperfections, for a final product that can appear cold and without depth. Sakano's mouth-blown glass, on the other hand, is beautifully rich and intense.

Glass
Engraver

omas Tisch Studio
99 Van Brunt Street, Suite 10B
ooklyn, NY 11231
8 643 9028
ww.tomastisch.org

Born into a rich legacy of Austrian glassmakers, Tomas Tisch trained at his family's glass studio in Salzburg. He attended art school in Vienna, and later studied at the Visual Studies Workshop in Rochester, New York. After focusing on photography and art, and then studying under very traditional teaching methods, he turned back to his original glass training. This time, however, he was on a mission to reinvent the age-old craft and to elevate it to a new level in the United States. He established his first studio in 1979 in Oakland, California, and now works from his own studio in Brooklyn, New York. Its arched windows offer a spectacular view of the Statue of Liberty.

As far as Tisch knows, he is the only artisan in New York still making wheel-cut glass, which had its heyday in the Victorian era when highly ornamental glassware was à la mode. In seventeenth-century France, it was used to decorate mirrors. The practice itself traces back more than 4,000 years, to the ancient Egyptians who first discovered how to grind gemstones to fashion decorative jewelry. While glass was once a rarity and a sign of one's wealth, the industrial revolution and mass production made such luxuries readily available.

Tisch has worked with an apprentice, Van Bilek, for five years. Tisch sits at a large, heavy wheel, focusing light on the piece of glass. Most of the tools in the studio come from Europe, and none of them are still being produced. The work is slow and very detail oriented, and the men must stop frequently and make adjustments to cut just the right design into the glass. Tisch has designed glassware for Steuben, the American glass brand, and Lobmeyr, a two-hundred-year-old Austrian company.

Tisch relishes collaborations, for the way they push him as an artist. High-profile decorators, including Albert Hadley, Peter Marino, and Philippe Starck, each of whom has a completely different style, trust him. For Tisch, glass is a seductive material. Even after all of these years, he still enjoys the challenge of working it as well as the precision required to achieve the desired result.

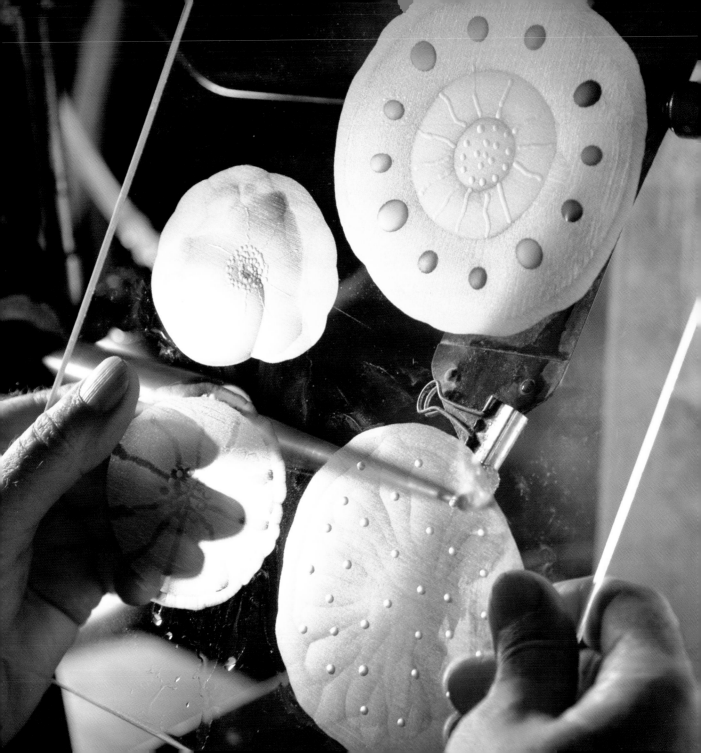

Glover

aniel Storto
North Main Street
loversville, NY 12078
8 725 4803
ww.danielstorto.com

Through the early part of the twentieth century, Gloversville, New York, had an active, almost urban feel thanks to its position along the Mohawk railroad line between Scotia and Grand Central Terminal. It was known as the glove capital of the world, as well as a center for the early movie industry. Its aptly named Glove Theatre served as host to movie premieres, often before they opened in California. Today, most storefronts in town are closed, making Daniel Storto's solitary glove atelier, next to the old theater, seem like it's on the set of an old movie. He grew up in this town, in an Italian family that was always sewing and tailoring, and now lives across the street from his studio. He is the last glover in Gloversville.

Something about leather intrigues Storto because of the unique challenges it presents that are not found with other materials. He learned how to work with leather at an early age from his grandfather, a shoemaker, and then he studied the anatomy of the hand. He started to collect gloves, and he now owns more than 5,000 pairs. He particularly admires styles from the 1940s and 1950s, and the way stitches were done at the time. In 1982, Storto moved to Los Angeles to work in costumes for movie studios. However, after sixteen years on the West Coast, he remained focused on his glove making, so returned to Gloversville—where everyone else's glove businesses had closed when work was outsourced to China—and set up shop.

Storto is eccentric, with an impeccable sense of style. His narrow atelier feels more like a jewelry shop, but lined with glove molds, tools, threads, needles, and leather—everything he is using at the time. It can take him up to five years to create a new design, each made one at a time. Recently, he experimented with typing on leather, trying to print a story onto skin.

Storto's gloves are never lined; he says leather is what people love, so why feel a lining instead? Lambskin, the best from France, Italy, and Switzerland, is his material of choice, because he can still find skins in the perfect color. He works like an architect sculpting a form, and the result is three-dimensional: the way the gloves are cut, individually stamped, and finished by rolling. Sometimes his gloves appear to be square or circular, but once they are on his clients' hands, they fill out beautifully. His work is featured in fashion magazines and exhibitions, and coveted by designers such as Dries Van Noten.

Hatter

Rod Keenan
02 West 122nd Street
ew York, NY 10027
12 678 9275
ww.rodkeenannewyork.com

Those looking to have a hat like one worn by a star need only to make an appointment at Rod Keenan's Harlem studio. His creations have been featured in major fashion magazines, donned by a wide range of celebrities, and carried at Barneys.

When other milliners wanted to go into the women's hat business, Keenan decided to turn his attention to men. He started simply, making hats for his friends, until demand grew for him to make a living from it.

His studio, a long, sunny space in the basement of a town house, is located in the heart of Harlem. A showroom displaying his designs is up front, and a workroom is in the back. The space brims with hat blocks, stands, pins, fabrics, straw, needles, buttons, and irons. Keenan makes two collections a year, straw for summer and felt for winter, as well as frequent custom orders.

Milliners are foremost dependent on materials: if the past season's weather wasn't good for the straw crop, they can't create a decent hat. Felt is harder to work with because of its weight. Keenan makes each hat individually, so no two are alike. He starts by fitting and wetting the form on a hat block. Once the form is dry, he begins cutting it with special scissors; then he irons, steams, and sews it by hand. Next comes the embellishing with ribbons, wool, and colorful thread. Keenan carries a meter stick at every stage to ensure the right measurements are maintained. While many companies have outsourced clothing making to China, and other millinery trades are dying, hat making is still an active business in New York—and Keenan has the goods to prove it.

ephen T. Anderson
7 3rd Avenue
onx, NY 10451
319 0815
w.stephentanderson.com

A client once presented Stephen T. Anderson with an old Chanel suit, which she wished to be transformed into one of his hand-hooked rugs. His original studio/showroom was located on First Avenue in Manhattan, but while the showroom remains, he has since moved his studio to a sun-filled ex-factory in the Bronx. Today, Anderson designs for all styles, deriving many of his patterns from quilts, which he transforms into modern styles.

Hand-hooked rugs originated in the United States and then the craft moved to Europe. Initially, the rage was to copy Aubusson carpets until the unique look of hand hooking found its own prized aesthetic. Underscoring his passion, Anderson is also a dealer of antique carpets.

Anderson's clients have included legendary designers such as the late Mark Hampton and Jay Johnson. He's always welcomed the end client, too; once, an advertising executive asked him to create a rug especially for his dog. Anderson starts designing every carpet with a hand drawing, and even though the carpets have a repetitive pattern, they never look exactly the same. He is careful to avoid uniformity, and, after another artisan works on a few squares in a panel, he moves on to another carpet. Anderson has also created pieces using clothing (such as the Chanel suit), but it is very labor intensive.

To make a carpet, Anderson first dyes the fabric and cuts it into strips six to eight inches long, using a "fettuccine machine." With a hook machine, he then follows a pattern that he has drawn and painted on the canvas. He used to work with burlap and hemp, but Anderson now prefers to work with linen, which is also the original material used in hand hooking.

Standing close together around the loom is a group of women, each with one hand under the rug pinching the fabric, and the other hand grabbing it on the top. Next to them, more women cut the fabric on top to create a uniform surface. The rugs are made in the same way as a century ago, except, Anderson says, he is constantly adjusting the sizes as orders keep getting bigger and bigger to suit today's homes.

he Gorst Studio
0 Harrison Avenue
arrison, NY 10528
4 815 0996
ww.gorststudio.com

While studying for her BFA at Cooper Union, Karen Gorst took a course in calligraphy and meditation, which she thought she'd never use. In her first calligraphy job, she tried to match a color to repair a damaged medieval manuscript; the process took more than two years. From that, a new interest was born: studying illumination, the effect of light and shadow on color, and combining it with her calligraphy work. With her passion for medieval art techniques and her calligraphy and illumination skills, Gorst received a grant from the French government to teach the art of illumination. Although she's done restoration work for the Metropolitan Museum of Art and the Cloisters Museum and Gardens, she now focuses primarily on creating original pieces for private clients.

Her studio, filled with tools and samples, resembles a medieval alchemy shop. A jar contains a wing so she can choose the appropriate quill for any project. A fridge is filled with paints. She makes glue from fish bones or aloe, and concocts color from vegetable sources.

Gorst's work is time consuming, so she listens attentively to her clients' stories and ideas. First, she must find the right-size parchment for the project. She prefers to work with handmade papers, as they are more forgiving with color. She has handful of papermakers with whom she regularly works. Gorst uses medieval color on every piece of illumination; each work is embossed and hand-carved when necessary. Mostly, she makes her own lettering fonts. For decorated letters, she creates a black line of powder, applies her own glue or gesso and gilding, and, finally, paints over each letter. Each project can take from two weeks to two years to complete, depending on the subject of the work. To each one she brings an understanding of paper, ink, and medieval techniques, and continues to find a legion of followers in our contemporary world. She also enjoys teaching and offers private workshops.

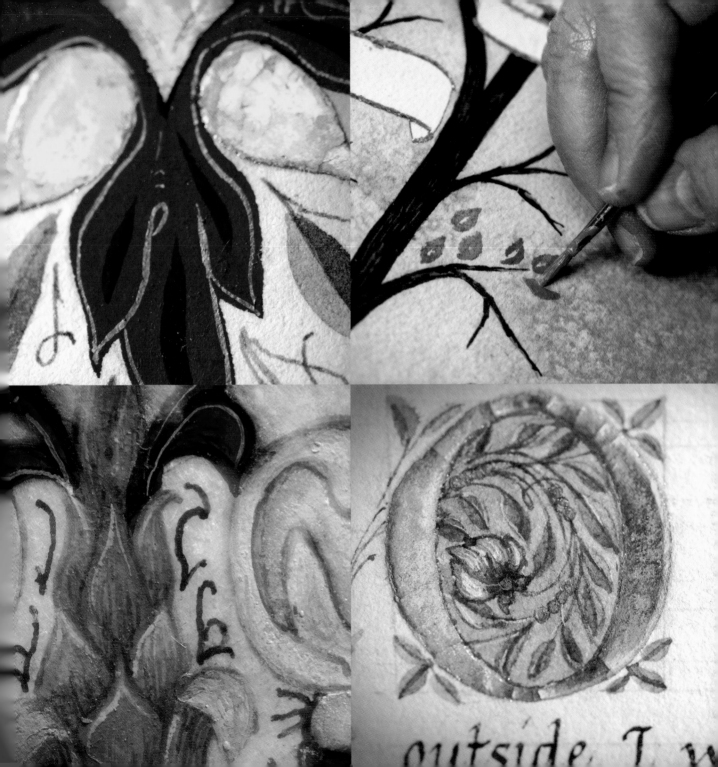

outside I w

Lacquerer

Nancy Lorenz
5 West 36th Street
New York, NY 10018
212 989 1354
www.nancy-lorenz.com

Nancy Lorenz's high school years in Japan greatly affected her aesthetic sensibility, but she never realized her appreciation for the culture would so infuse her career as a lacquerer. After graduating high school, Nancy studied painting and printmaking at the University of Michigan, and then moved to Rome where she discovered an interest in gilding. Eventually, she opened her own restoration business in New York, although she continued to work as an artist as well. Next door to her first studio was the office of interior designer Bill Sofield, with whom she often worked. This collaboration led to work with other interior designers and, ultimately, private clients.

While lacquerwork originated in China, it was the Japanese who transformed it into an art form. Lacquerwork first arrived in the courts of Europe when trade routes opened in the eighteenth century, and it soon became à la mode. It reached popularity again during the 1930s Art Deco movement.

Lacquer used to be made by heating the extremely toxic secretion found between larvae eggs in an insect shell, but since the 1930s, most lacquerwork has been synthetic—the famously shiny surface fashioned with a paint gun. Today, the look is achieved with shellac.

Inspired by her dreams and travels, Lorenz's studio is filled with mother-of-pearl raindrops and organic shapes in gold leaf. Every time she completes a project, she mounts a sample from the work onto a small piece of wood, which serves as inspiration for other clients. She prefers to craft her own tools, and she uses them to make her uniquely formulated gesso of rabbit glue and chalk. This gesso is then applied to the wood in fine layers. The gesso must be just the right temperature because when it cools, it is sanded to achieve the ideal smoothness. Next, Lorenz takes a piece of mother-of-pearl from a large stack, cuts it into shapes, and adorns it with gold leaf. A completed piece often requires forty time-consuming steps, each one steeped in tradition. The finish of each piece seems to change continually in the light. A surface that starts cold immediately warms under one's touch, feeling almost like silk.

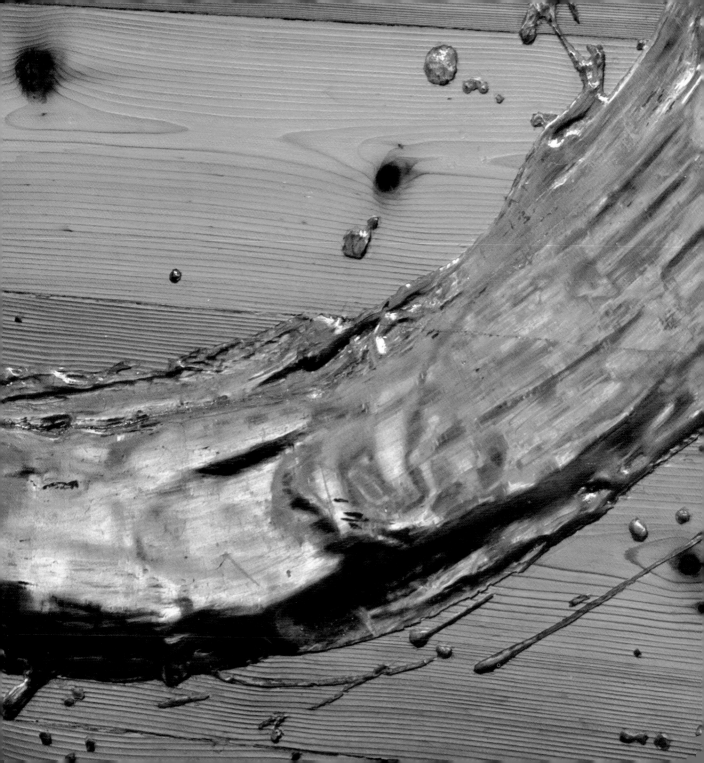

**Letterpress
Printer**

BE JEALOUS. BE HAP...

...OTTEN. DO GOOD ANY...

...ENOUGH. GIVE YOUR BEST A...

...VAY- IT IS ALWAYS ABOUT US...

...PEACE WITHIN OURSELV...

ayspace
24 Third Street, Studio E104
ooklyn, NY 11215
3 596 3520
vw.swayspace.cvom

Letterpress was the prevalent form of printing that started around the time of Johannes Gutenberg's invention of the printing press in the late fifteenth century, and remained widely used for books through the early twentieth century. Now, the rare letterpress is used only for formal invitations or the occasional business card. Longtime friends Patrick Fenton and Willy Schwenzfeier, who have backgrounds in visual communications and product design, respectively, happened onto letterpress when they found one for sale in Williamsburg, Brooklyn. They restored it, learned how to use it, and started a business, Swayspace, in 2002. They now run a large operation at the Can Factory in Brooklyn, which is filled with boxes of lead and wood type as well as several letterpress machines, some of which are more than one hundred years old.

Letterpress is not an inexpensive printing solution. A visit to the Swayspace studio, or even the company website, reveals creative samples they've created for artists, corporations, and private clients—and, yes, lots of invitations. Graphic designers help to make initial designs on paper, and then select the ink colors. Next, they mix the colors, select the fonts and typography, customize the design, and choose the paper stock. What underlines Swayspace's work is the finished product's fun look: brighter, bolder colors than were ever available in Gutenberg's day, and a playful, offbeat aesthetic.

Many of the artisans at Swayspace have been there from the beginning, and are hooked on the time- and labor-intensive process. Some of the presses require not only enormous physical expenditures to operate but also the ability to perform repetitive movement consistently. Along with Fenton and Schwenzfeier, the artisans get satisfaction from seeing cards and invitations—each one a work of art—rolling out of the machine.

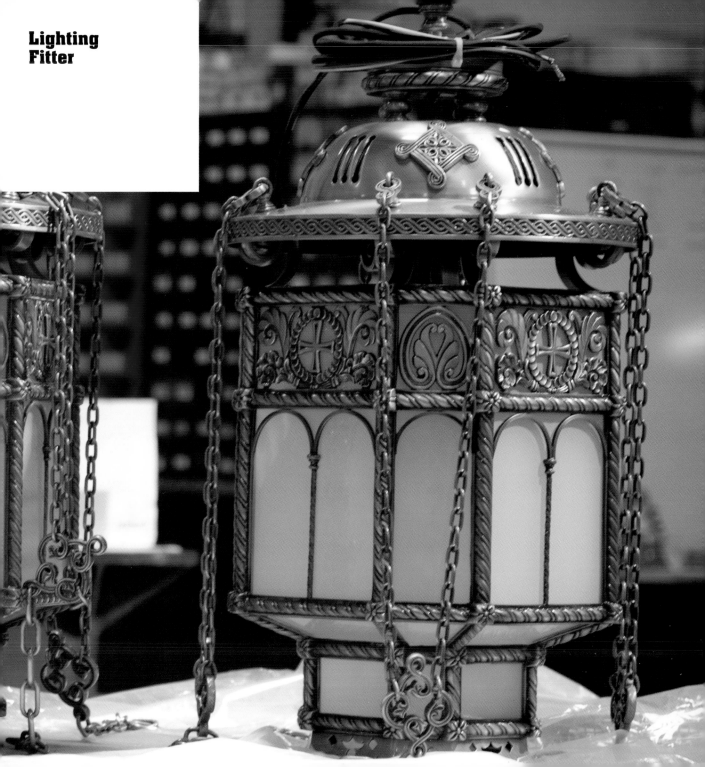

Rambusch Lighting
160 Cornelison Avenue
Jersey City, NJ 07302
1 333 2525
www.rambusch.com

Started in 1898, Rambusch is a family-owned company that is now run by brothers Edwin and Martin, whose parents also still work in the business. The company has two specializations: lighting, which produces custom designs; and crafts, which encompasses decorative metalwork and stained glass.

Rambusch's lighting department was born when tungsten-filament lights were first created as the primary source of interior illumination. This division set out to refine and elevate the new technology. During a 1908 visit to Philadelphia's Cathedral Basilica of Saints Peter and Paul, Forde Rambusch noticed the glare of a single, suspended electric light, which prevented him from admiring the murals his own family business's crafts division had created. He developed a repoussé metal "shield" around the bulb that directed the light source to the paintings rather than straight into the eyes of the worshipers. Since then, the company's creations have ranged from simple lanterns to highly intricate luminaries.

Edwin and Martin consider themselves stewards of artistic traditions, and are proud to say that Rambusch will implement and evoke the appropriate style to a particular project, including existing architecture. Their flexibility and ability to work in various mediums and to implement different techniques are matched in their commitment to the collaborative process—there's never a standout, boldfaced designer who steals the credit. Whether in the office or the atelier, everyone works together closely, mimicking the family nature of the company.

Rambusch doesn't just make a light, it makes a light to fit the needs of its clients, ranging from cultural institutions, such as the Museum of Modern Art, to public spaces like Jazz at Lincoln Center, to private homes in New York and across the United States. They keep drawings from past projects on file, which eases the first steps of a repeat project or renovation, and gives their library the feel of a historic survey of American decorative styles.

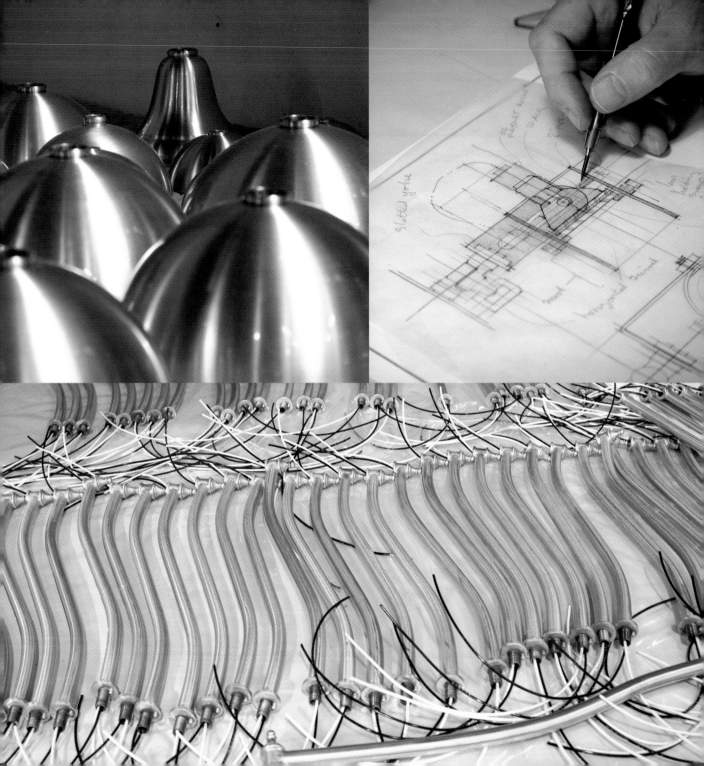

Luthier

thaniel Rowan
2 3rd Street, Studio E101
ooklyn, NY 11215
:rowan@earthlink.net

The first musical instrument that eighteen-year-old Nathaniel Rowan made was a banjo, which was part of his violin training at school in Red Wing, Minnesota. After studying the techniques of various American and European violin makers, he apprenticed in Salt Lake City with top luthiers, or violin makers. In 1997, he moved to New York City and toiled in several shops, including seven years with David Segal Violins Ltd.

In 2005, Rowan established his own studio in Brooklyn, where he spends months working on each instrument. He believes a true violin is "alive," and that his European spruce and bass woods—along with the occasional piece salvaged from the street—must settle before they can be shaped. Traditionally, violins have four strings, but Rowan has modernized this form, and prefers to make instruments with five strings. Although he understands that some musicians are more willing to experiment than others, he hopes that with the evolution of music, more people will begin to appreciate variations on the norm.

Rowan customizes violins with different finishes, and—as he continues to refine his alchemy—makes varnishes by hand when he visits his parents in the North Country. Everything else about his craft is rooted in tradition. Even when one of Rowan's violins appears to be structurally complete, it isn't quite ready. For a full year, he attunes the newly fashioned instrument to changes in the weather and seasons, tests its sound quality, and monitors its maturing varnish.

**Mannequin
Maker**

Ralph Pucci
West 18th Street
New York, NY 10011
633 0452
www.ralphpucci.net

The word "mannequin" comes from the Dutch *mannekijn*, or "little man," and was first used to demonstrate how fabrics draped on the human form. In 1976, Ralph Pucci asked his parents, who had been running a successful mannequin business since the 1950s, if he could start to manufacture his own figures. His approach was architectural, which can be seen in his first collaboration with designer Andrée Putman in 1985. He continues to show mannequins in his enormous gallery in Manhattan's Flatiron District.

From the beginning, he has challenged the notion that mannequins are merely functional displays. Fashion designer Anna Sui first approached Pucci before the opening of her inaugural boutique in 1992. She had always collected antique hat forms and wanted to incorporate them in the new space. Anna and some of her friends created dozens of papier-mâché "Dolly heads," which Pucci still makes for her stores. Another successful collection was with the colorful Blank Kids. Inspired by the early work of Keith Haring and contemporary Japanese artists such as Takashi Murakami, Ralph Pucci's figures, in multiple shapes and colors, were displayed alongside giant totems by illustrator Michael Bartolos. In addition, Chesley McLaren, who started her career as a graphic designer on Seventh Avenue in Manhattan's Fashion District, translated her whimsical French style to the "New Couture" collection for Ralph Pucci.

While Ralph Pucci's innovative mannequins have captivated the interest of a truly creative clientele, his collaborator Robert Clyde Anderson's figures are so realistic people have been known to strike up conversations with them. Most of Anderson's hand-painted designs are of men and women in their twenties and thirties with long, chiseled features. Ralph Pucci's personal favorite, however, is an older couple in their sixties. "They're often overlooked in retail, though," he jokes.

In recent decades, Pucci has become the man to know in the design world: a curator of sorts who never rests on his success; a man whose stable of talent includes some of the best names in furniture and decorative arts, such as Hervé van der Straeten, Patrick Naggar, and Vladimir Kagan.

Metalsmith

es Métalliers Champenois
 2nd Avenue
aterson, NJ 07514
'3 279 3573
ww.l-m-c.com

In 1986, Jean Wiart, one of four partners in Les Métalliers Champenois (LMC), arrived in New York City from France to restore the flame and torch of the Statue of Liberty. He came with trunkloads of tools and a few tons of materials, and because of subsequent demand for his skills, he and his wife never left. Since then, he has done work for the Metropolitan Museum of Art, the New York Police Building, and the New York Public Library, as well as private homes and projects for artist Louise Bourgeois.

With its workshop of modern equipment, centuries-old anvils, coal forges, gas, and tools, LMC works with pure aluminum, bronze, copper, iron, steel, and titanium. The company is one of the few large-scale producers of repoussé work in the world. Repoussé is the art of making intricate three-dimensional shapes from flat pieces of metal using only one's hands, an anvil, and several dozen different hammers.

LMC's repoussé atelier features walls covered with new and antique hammers. In the studio toils a mechanic named William Peyny, who arrived from France in 1995 with a degree in ironwork. In a matter of minutes, his rough hands tap a metal blank into a magnificently detailed oak leaf. Recently, LMC labored on a gate bound for one of the grand houses along the bluff in Newport, Rhode Island; in total, the project took at least 25,000 hours to complete.

LMC's showroom offers examples of the company's work, including a space filled with detailed, freehand drawings of every project. These drawings form an extensive archive, and help to further LMC's commitment to continuing the tradition of fine ornamental metalwork in America. The company is a registered member of the National Apprenticeship Program, each year welcoming apprentices from all over the world then honing their skills to ensure the trade lives on. Wiart, along with the four other partners, Julien Legeard, Jean-Paul Dorieux, Vincent Thomas, and Zoltan Kovacs, think of LMC as a family. The walls contain pictures of employees taken each year at Saint Eloi, where they go to celebrate the work of the year. As Wiart says, "I am an average man who makes extraordinary work."

Mosaicist

Gregory Muller Associates
5 Kent Avenue
Brooklyn, NY 11211
3 599 6220
www.gregorymullerassoc.com

Gregory Muller is an artist by trade, who ended up as a designer of mosaics simply because he was asked to make one. He trained under three generations of sculptors, learned the technical aspects of the craft in Italy and Greece, and then opened his New York City studio in 1989.

Adjacent to his studio is a room where stone can be cut to his precise needs, or into strips, and then "guillotined" or clipped to the proper thickness. He selects each piece of granite, marble, or onyx from the quarry. His team has designed and fabricated bathtubs, columns, fireplaces, fountains, furniture, and sinks.

The artisans' first step is to create a drawing of the intended design, which is then translated into a pattern on a computer by Muller's brother, Alex. This pattern is then printed in the correct scale and color, and a sample is sent to the client for approval. Muller's artistic background is evident in his strong sense of color. The team includes three women, Ewa, Malgorzata, and Martina, and for very large projects they enlist the help of art-school students.

Muller's studio is lined with strips of stonework, arranged according to color. Its walls display drawings and patterns of the team's current and past projects. An enormous table, necessary for some of the large-scale installations, looms over the space. Because of the weight of stone, the studio was designed so that a truck can come directly inside to pick up a job.

Work produced by Gregory Muller and Associates can be found in homes across the United States, and though the team prefers to work in its studio, sometimes it must create installations onsite to achieve the client's desired quality, look, and feel.

Neon
Fabricator

te Brite Neon
2 3rd Street
ooklyn, NY 11215
8 855 6082
ww.litebriteneon.com

Art installations, beer signs, and window displays all show the handiwork of Matt Dilling and his team at Lite Brite Neon. On two floors of the old Can Factory near the Gowanus Canal in Brooklyn, the team transforms just about any drawing into neon lights. Artists, fashion designers, museums, and restaurants all rely on their skills. In the office meeting room in the middle of the floor, Dilling, who sports John Lennon glasses, helps clients to stretch their imagination and color palette.

The space brims with colored glass tubes ready to be cleaned, bent, and filled with neon. First, Dilling forms the desired shape, seals its ends, and initiates a series of complex processes to remove any impurities. Then, he adds electrodes and "bombards," or heats the insides to almost 400 degrees Celsius, which causes an electric current to pass through. Next, he pumps gas into the tube at low pressure; the color of the neon depends on the recipe of gases used, whether argon, helium, mercury, or phosphorous. The glass tubes then undergo an aging process, which ensures that the gases will be stable for a long time. Finally, the tubes get mounted according to the sign or installation specifications.

Downstairs, in a cavernous space—sandwiched between giant cutting tools for the glass tubes—is a huge storage area and showroom. Neon light making is still done completely by hand, and even though a lot of production has been outsourced to China, Lite Brite Neon's business is booming. The company retains a certain allure among those who appreciate the quality of their neon. Clients also come here to rent a sign or to buy a ready-made one on display. Lite Brite's lights usually work for forty years, with minor repairs, which the team will gladly make, always happy to see their work again.

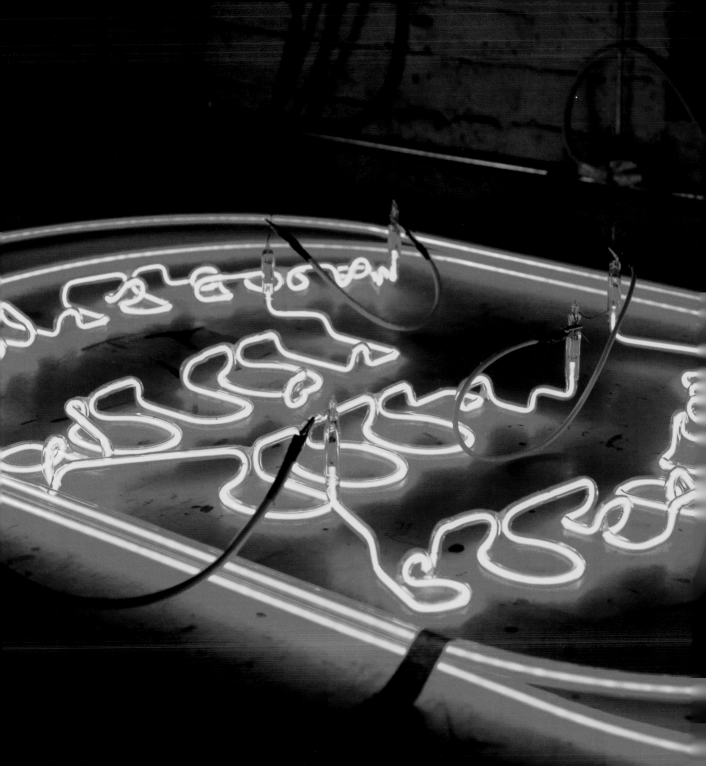

Papermaker

eu Donné
5 West 36th Street
ew York, NY 10018
2 226 0573
ww.dieudonne.org

Located in the Fashion District of Manhattan, nonprofit Dieu Donné has been dedicated to the art of paper since 1976. The company is committed to "the creation, promotion, and preservation of new contemporary art using the hand-papermaking process." Artistic director Paul Wong has been a part of this mission since Dieu Donné's founding, by Sue Gosin and Bruce Weinburg, and says the paper mill is able to help artists, both emerging and seasoned, innovate the medium.

Papermaking has a long history in American art, especially in the Arts and Crafts period. Artists such as Elbert Hubbard and Douglas Howell are credited with "bridging the craft and fine art of papermaking so that the medium and the message became indistinguishable." Browse the upstairs gallery and you'll see just how far the boundaries of the medium can be pushed—is that really paper? Fibers include cotton, linen, flax, even abaca, and incredible variations of opacity and thickness. Recent shows featured work by Michele Oka Doner and William Kentridge.

Downstairs, Dieu Donné also serves as an educational facility, offering workshops for adults at both introductory and advanced levels. If you haven't taken an art class lately, you'll be amazed at the endless possibilities for the material: once you've mastered how to make paper, you can stencil or watermark it, or perhaps tackle embedding other materials within it, and then add a dimension to it with mold casting. In 1990, the Workspace Program was created, which awards annual residencies to emerging artists to create handmade work in paper.

There is a sense of collaboration, encouragement, and process throughout the 7,000-square-foot facility, which has worked with leading artists such as Louise Bourgeois, Kiki Smith, Glenn Ligon, and Chuck Close, who serves on its board of advisors. Art institutions and publishers, too, such as the Whitney Museum of American Art Library and Pace Prints, rely on Dieu Donné's work for special editions. The company also produces custom paper for purchase by artists, whether for photography, drawing, painting, or museum archiving, with sheets as large as seven by ten feet.

Piano
Maker

einway & Sons
teinway Place
ng Island City, NY 11105
3 721 2600
ww.steinway.com

In the early twentieth century, piano making was a major industry. The Steinway family, a fixture of New York social life, founded the Steinway Company in 1873. Steinway is the only piano-making company that remains in business in New York, and until a few years ago, original family members were still involved in the operations. In its heyday, Steinway was producing 150 pianos each year; today, that number is far fewer, but the instruments are still crafted in exactly the same way as they were more than a century ago, each one requiring nearly a year to complete.

Steinway has two New York locations, one in Manhattan and the other on eleven acres in Queens, plus a factory in Hamburg, Germany. There are six different Steinway models; each one is made from approximately 12,000 parts, not including screws or metal in the rim. The basic woods are derived from across the United States and Canada, while the exotic ones used for the veneers—Bubinga, Ceylon satinwood, cherry, figured maple, iced birch, Macassar ebony, mahogany, and walnut—come from all over the world.

One thing that sets Steinway apart is the way its craftsmen bend the piano's outer case: they invented the process. The so-called "bent rim" is what lends the instruments not only their beautiful tone but also their strength. The ritual of bending the wood and gluing the hard maple wood rim together takes place every morning at the same time. The twenty-minute process involves six people—and a lot of glue. To ensure the wood is completely free of humidity, each newly bent piano body rests for at least six weeks before the next step. The veneer is then cut from a machine that dates to 1871.

The Steinway factory is enormous, with each floor and room used for a different purpose: adjusting, bending, conditioning, exotic finishing, painting, polishing, and tuning. The tuning process starts with a machine but is finished by hand to ensure correctness. Women, who are considered to be more precise in their work, run the polishing and action rooms. Every time a piano completes a stage in the process, it is moved from one room to the next, and a detailed checklist is updated.

Steinway runs the largest piano-making apprenticeship program in the United States. Each apprentice learns all of the processes, and then moves on to the department where he or she shows the most promise. Some of the employees, graduates of the apprenticeship program, have been with Steinway for more than forty years.

Pleater

Entering Harry's Pleating & Stitch, located on the third floor of a building in Manhattan's Fashion District, is like stepping back in time: here, visitors find an old pleating machine, steam oven, and cardboard patterns designed by the company's original owner, from whom Harry Harhar purchased the business. A large table looms over the space and sewing machines sit at the rear. Harhar, his wife, Suzanna, and his seven artisans learned their skills on the job. In this studio, the men focus on the pleating, since it is extremely physical work that requires them to be on their feet all day, and the women handle the sewing, which is the detailed, manual work.

The pattern that makes the mold is drawn by hand onto two very large pieces of cardboard. Some of the molds have been used for decades. The two sides of the mold, which are mirror images, are laid open on a table and the fabric gets sandwiched between them. Using the right amount of fabric and pressing it with the right tension is critical, as this is what achieves the desired pleat. Closing the pattern requires the work of a few men to tie the knots and secure the compression. Next, the men carry the bundle to a steam box where the fabrics steam at 60 degrees C. for a few minutes, depending on the type of fabric (while polyester holds the best pleats, not every fabric can be pleated) and the desired design. After each roll cools off, the mold is carefully opened. It's still very hot, and can't be touched for a few minutes, as the blanket of steam escapes. The smell is powerful, and each fabric has a unique perfume. Once at room temperature, the women's work begins: they sew the pressed pleats into place, according to the designer's specifications. Pleating is definitive and errors cannot be disguised. Only one piece of fabric can be pleated at a time. Then the cardboard designs are rolled back up, secured by a ribbon, and left to await their next job.

While pleating was extremely fashionable in the time of Madame Viollet and her plissé dresses in the early twentieth century, it had become a dying art until recently when—to Harry Harhar's delight—a handful of young fashion designers, such as Jason Wu, began rediscovering the beauty of pleats.

Quilter

Julie Floersch
5 West 36th Street, Suite 11C
New York, NY 10018
646 338 3272
www.juliefloersch.com

Julie Floersch arrived in New York City a decade ago, studied at the Fashion Institute of Technology for two years, and had ambitions of being a fashion designer. Growing up, she always loved sewing and creating intricate patterns, which seemed like the appropriate career path. After stints at J. Crew and Ralph Lauren, where she made patterns and technical design drawings, Floersch struck out on her own, inspired by quilting and her ability to create textiles and three-dimensional multimedia works, such as beading, embroidery, and sharpie drawings.

Her debut quilt took more than two years to complete and was made up of 5,000 pieces, all sewn by hand. She now works square by square, primarily in denim, and recently created a portrait entirely out of old jeans. Her windowless shoebox-sized studio in Brooklyn is often filled with friends she's enlisted to help her pull together the thousands of fabric pieces required for each quilt.

Quilting is considered a traditional craft with humble beginnings; many believe it started centuries ago, when women began piecing together leftover scraps of material used to make bed coverings. However, quilts and their fine needlework have had an alluring history, ranging from decorative objects, to signs of an owner's wealth, to functional, omnipresent items during the Civil War. With the advent of Singer sewing machines in the mid-1800s—and their accessibility to the masses through installment payments—quilting experienced wild popularity as clothing making became both easier and faster, leaving women more free time for quilting as a pastime.

Energetic and creative, Floersch often wears fabric jewelry inspired by her quilts. In her hands, a mere sketch is transformed to massive effect. First, she makes an enlarged photocopy of the sketch, then she traces over it. Next, she cuts each shape, which she lays onto a piece of fabric or denim. Finally, she stitches together these puzzlelike pieces, creating a patchwork, which she fills with organic cotton batting and closes with a unique backing, completing the fiber art.

Sculptural Metalsmith

Kammetal
Seabring Street
Brooklyn, NY 11231
718 722 7400
www.kammetal.com

Set off on a quiet street and housed behind a small green door, Kammetal makes a big impression with its noise. The warehouse space contains state-of-the-art lasers, water jets, and old metalworking instruments: bending machines, grinding machines, sanding blocks, and welding machines. Sam Kusack runs the studio with his brother and a crew of ten; the team realizes just about any form, ranging from a staircase to a work of art, in any metal, from aluminum to brass to stainless steel. Kusack's clients include architects, contemporary artists, furniture designers, restaurants, and even retail stores. But the studio's specialty is foundry work for artists. Using high-pressure water and sand, its computer-run machines can cut through metal as thick as five inches.

Kusack is an extremely articulate, tall young man with smiling eyes. He went to Cooper Union and worked for an artist before starting Kammetal. His soft-spoken demeanor makes visitors feel as though everything he's doing is simple, whether buying sophisticated equipment, running the company, or creating a massive installation. He does part of his work by computer, part on machinery, and the rest by hand—it's exactly this combination of artisan skill and technology that he finds so fascinating about his craft.

CH Marine Yachts
Cartwright Road
Shelter Island, NY 11964
631 584 2231
www.chmarineyachts.com

It might not be his biggest claim to fame, but Billy Joel has a lot to do with the success of CH Marine. Tucked away on Shelter Island, Peter Needham and his team have been building custom yachts since 1979. They have made dozens of boats, including one for the Piano Man. Not too long ago, there were numerous boat builders along the New York shoreline; now, theirs is one of just a few. Needham says CH Marine has survived thanks in no small part to Joel, who is a patron client. Joel came by frequently when they were building his yacht, as clients are invited to do, and, fascinated by the process and caliber of work, has lent his name ever since, becoming almost a de facto spokesman.

CH Marine's yachts are made to suit any requirement or recreational pursuit: fishing, scuba diving, or simple family-outing cruising. Needham will help with the design and be there every step of the way, until the final "promenade" with the boat and owner. He's the first to say he gets attached to each vessel over the eight weeks on average it takes to build one, wishing it did not have to leave the marina.

Each yacht is completely custom built, from cockpit layout to upholstery color. Many of the artisans at work in the carpentry shop are former custom furniture makers, which accounts for the level of detail in their work. There are also painters and fiberglass specialists, as well as licensed electricians who work on wiring for the systems in an off-site atelier. The varnishing room is arguably the busiest, with all sorts of knobs and doors being varnished and sanded—a process that is repeated with about fifteen coats, and needs to be redone every year to combat saltwater corrosion. The teak is hand selected and rubbed by hand with traditional tung oil varnish, and the hull is made from a Kevlar-fiberglass concoction. Even the hardware can be unique to each boat: 316 stainless-steel chocks, no problem! So it should come as no surprise that most of their creations are still in the hands of the original owners, including Joel's.

Silversmith

lentin Yotkov
Jay Street, Suite 210
ooklyn, NY 11201
852 8640
w.valentinyotkov.com

As a child in Bulgaria, Valentin Yotkov wrote poetry. One day, his teacher called his mother to say that he should be doing even more artistic work. He began to draw, and eventually studied ceramics, glass blowing, and woodcarving, until a visit to a museum inspired him to become a silversmith.

The only way to learn the craft was to be in a guild, so Yotkov approached a legendary silversmith and asked if he could be his apprentice. This master craftsman became a father figure to Yotkov as well. The apprentice was a natural, but after gaining great success, he was ready for something new. In 1990, Yotkov moved to the United States to gain more freedom in his work; he brought along his tools and his longtime assistant Sharon, but negligible English. He started a studio in Brooklyn, gained regular customers, and became a teacher himself. All of his work is on display— and for sale—in his studio.

Today, Yotkov also teaches chasing and repoussé work in his studio. These techniques originated millennia ago, and have roots in Bulgaria's Thracian gold treasures and fine silverwork. Yotkov's decade of training in the craft involved intense study of excavated Thracian metal artifacts; he learned how they were made and then modified the ancient tools and techniques to inform his own designs. These antiquities continue to inspire him to this day.

To start a new project, Yotkov "chases," or draws, lines on the front of a piece of metal (usually silver or gold). Next, he turns the piece over so that he can "punch" relief work through the back. Then he shapes and anneals the piece, and chases it once again before adhering stones or other decorative elements. By continuing the tradition of his native culture's timeless trade, Yotkov keeps the beauty of ancient Bulgarian crafts very much alive through his contemporary designs.

nturella Studio
 Union Square East, Suite 1110
w York, NY 10003
2 228 4252
ww.venturellastudio.com

Many people may not be familiar with Florida's Morse Museum, but a visit to Venturella Studio will likely reveal part of its legendary collection of Tiffany glass awaiting repair or restoration. Thomas Venturella opened his studio in 1985 after studying painting at the School of the Art Institute of Chicago and receiving a BFA from the University of Chicago. A lifelong interest in glass and the way light affects it, as well as an apprenticeship learning the craft, led to a position as a senior conservator of glass at the Metropolitan Museum of Art.

Louis Comfort Tiffany is still the name most synonymous with glass art. After Tiffany traveled in Europe and developed an affinity for medieval art, he devoted himself to finding a way to improve the coloration and 3-D capacity of stained glass. He invented techniques that started a revolution in the field, including drapery, favrille, fracture, opalescent, ring mottle, ripple, and streamer varieties.

Venturella's studio, off Union Square, feels like a church: his amalgamation of religious artifacts and saintly statues are everywhere. One wall features an impressive collection of glass waiting to be cut and shaped for work. Venturella starts each project offsite, where he takes measurements and makes sketches and drawings by hand. He has done work for Frank Lloyd Wright's Taliesin West, the Metropolitan Museum of Art, churches, universities, private collections, and, of course, the Morse Museum.

One of the biggest parts of any project is the research that precedes the work. First, he needs to find as many documents as possible to select individual pieces and colors with confidence. Back in the studio, Venturella draws a full-size cartoon and translates it into glass lead lines. He and his assistant trace the pattern onto each numbered piece of glass, select the colors, and cut the glass with a breaker-grozier plier. The cutting is all about pressure and control. A large piece of glass serves as an easel, as wax is poured over all of the pieces; this enables the artists to adjust the color, if necessary. Venturella and his assistant then fill lines with lead (for more classic, longer lines) or copper (for works with many small pieces). The glass must be of the highest quality, and since no one in the United States is making it as Tiffany used to, Venturella now imports it primarily from Europe.

Stonemason

Ottavino Corporation
-60 Pitkin Avenue
:one Park, NY 11417
B 848 9404
vw.ottavinostones.com

Founded by a monument carver in 1913, and staffed now by its third generation of stonemasons, the Ottavino company specializes in everything stone: from marble façade restorations, sculptures, and classical carvings, to grouting, fountain restoration, and the reparation and reconstruction of exterior stonewalls and towers. Ottavino has restored notable buildings throughout New York City, including the Whitney Museum of American Art, the Temple of Dendur at the Metropolitan Museum of Art, the New York Public Library, the Statue of Liberty, and Saint Patrick's Cathedral. The company's projects range from conserving park fountains, sculptures, and memorials to preserving civic monuments and institutions. Much of its work now focuses on making repairs that reflect changing geographical and climate needs. The Ottavinos believe that historic structures can be successfully preserved using nonintrusive techniques, and that any change should subtly blend into the appearance of an existing structure.

Stonemason, carver, and restorer Luis Batista has been a part of Ottavino for twenty-six years. He feels that a good craftsman has to "follow" the stone, as nature created it, to see how it reacts. He is so committed to and passionate about his trade, that when his day's work is done, he still keeps carving and etching stone at home.

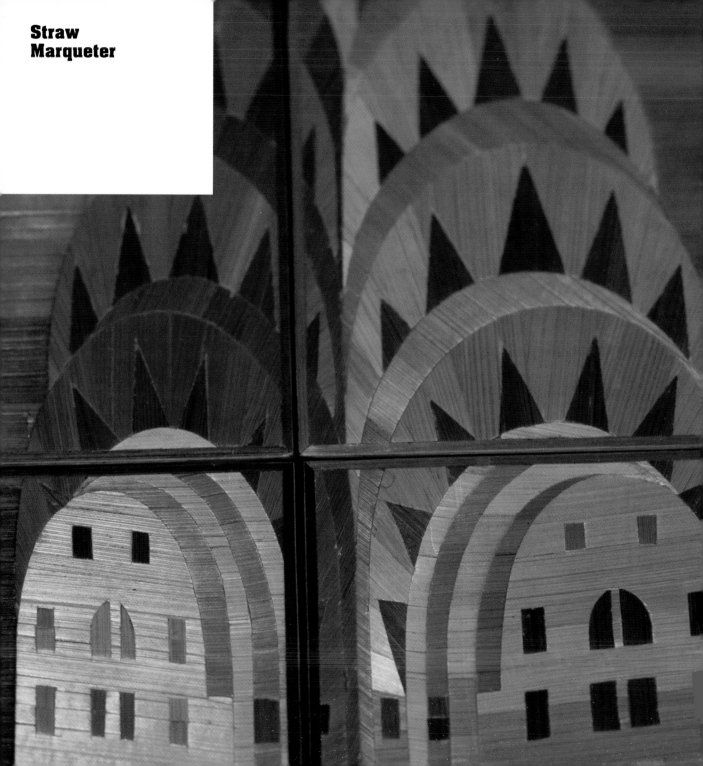

Straw
Marqueter

ndrine Viollet
5 Driggs Avenue
ooklyn, NY 11211
8 782 1727
w.atelierviollet.com

Straw marquetry is an art form that started in the court of Louis XV and became nearly obsolete until a brief resurrection by Jean-Michel Frank during the 1930s French Art Deco movement. Extremely delicate, the process involves opening and flattening individual sheaths of rye, oat, or wheat straw, and arranging them in elaborate patterns on boxes, decorative panels, furniture, and walls. The technique is simple but it must be executed perfectly, with no gaps between each straw. The straw is either applied directly onto wood, for simple patterns, or onto backing paper, for more intricate patterns. In the latter case, the desired pattern is cut with a razor blade and then applied to the wood. Next, the straw is waxed and polished. Subtle variations in the final product's color almost mimic painting: the clean lines and natural iridescence of straw, even when dyed in a natural palette, contribute to its allure.

Sandrine Viollet taught herself the craft of straw marquetry, through trying different techniques, developing a line of colors, and studying the antique marquetry boxes and objects she has collected. The high-quality rye straw she uses is imported from the Saône and Loire regions of France, where it is harvested specifically for the marquetry craft. She works on larger installations in her husband's furniture workshop in Brooklyn and on smaller ones in her home studio, where she keeps her dyes, straw, and the few basic tools she needs, including white glue and a unique instrument that she bought in England and uses to cut and open each sheath. Recently, having labored for an entire year on one project, she was awarded the Meilleur Ouvrier de France, the highest possible honor in an artistic field. Straw marquetry is a craft rooted in French history and one that Viollet is committed to evolving, across the Atlantic, for future generations.

**Tableware
Maker**

Sydney Albertini
519 Acabonac Road
East Hampton, NY 11937
631 907 9371
www.sydneyalbertini.com

Sydney Albertini has always been extremely creative, studying art at Paris's Atelier de Sèvres and frescoing for a year in Florence. She remembers painting on pottery as a young girl at her mother's store in Connecticut. When she was pregnant with her first child twelve years ago, she found herself craving a creative outlet as the chemicals in paints made painting prohibitive. She designed a plate with a forest pattern and it became an instant success. Anything she made sold immediately, and soon she considered herself more of a painter of pottery than canvas.

Albertini's studio and home lie on the Peconic Land Trust in East Hampton, Long Island. She lives with her three kids, dogs, and a cat in a quirky, blue-walled wood house filled with her paintings, quilts, and sewing projects. She does most of her work early in the morning so that she can take care of her kids.

One section of her studio contains stacked dishes waiting to be painted, some of which are handmade and others "raw ware" that she buys in Italy. She sketches on each piece in black pencil, but doesn't need to erase the lines because they burn off in the firing process. Once she has determined the design, she starts pushing and moving the paint around with a fine brush. She must work fast because the clay is porous and the paint dries quickly. Some paints don't mix well, so if she wants to adjust a color, she simply adds one on top of another—but no more than three layers or the design will be too thick and risk cracking the clay base when fired. She prefers to use crystal glazes on the back of her plates, which explode when fired, creating a unique patterned signature. She likes the mystery of not knowing what the finished piece will really look like until after the firing process, what might crack or how a hue might change.

Her colorful collection is sold at Barneys, although all of her work can be customized for special orders. For private clients—who love her offbeat designs— she regularly creates unique dinnerware patterns that require at least eight weeks to complete.

Tanner

ergamena
 Factory Street
ontgomery, NY 12549
5 649 5806
ww.pergamena.net

Parchment is basically leather subjected to chemical alterations that render it colorless and translucent. It was widely used after papyrus and before pulp paper became the predominant material for writing. The Meyer family, owners of Pergamena, a handmade parchment and tanning company, has roots in leatherwork that trace back to 1550 in Germany.

Jesse Meyer, the son of the current patriarch, Karl Meyer, approached his father in 1999, wanting to develop a new branch of the parchment-producing business. The younger Meyer had studied sculpture but decided it would be too hard to live as an artist in New York City. He felt there was a demand for parchment, for use in bookbinding and furniture making. So he taught himself how to make it by reading books on medieval recipes and trolling the Internet. One thing he learned was that each animal produces a different type of parchment. Young goats, for example, yield a very fine parchment, which is ideal for calligraphy.

The first step to creating parchment is to remove the entire animal hide delicately, ensuring that the least amount of flesh remains attached. The skin must either be worked on immediately or properly preserved, or it will spoil. Hair is taken off of the outside of the skin using calcium carbonate; at the same time, the skin rotates continuously so that the chemical is evenly distributed. Next, the inside of the skin is fleshed and any remaining chemicals are washed off, rendering the skin pH-neutral. The damp skin is then left to dry flat on a rack. The neutral-color skins are simply hung to dry, yielding a stiff and shrunken, almost unrecognizable product. After the skin is partially rehydrated, it is stretched, sanded, and shaved to the appropriate texture: gloss, sheer, smooth, or velvet.

Meyer has become a bit of a legend in the business. He makes all of his stretching frames by hand for the most difficult part of the job: pulling the skin taut and screwing it into the frame. He feels lucky to be surrounded by history, helping bookbinders, furniture makers, and interior designers to create what they imagine. His father and brother, meanwhile, are still at working in the family's leather tannery.

**xtile Conservation
boratory**
e Cathedral of St. John the Divine
7 Amsterdam Avenue
w York, NY 10025
 316 7523
w.stjohndivine.org

In northern Manhattan, around the side of the magnificent Cathedral Church of St. John the Divine, a beautiful Greek Revival building contains a textile conservation center. Marlene Eidelheit directs this studio, located in the cathedral's old orphanage, which overlooks a serene garden. The cathedral was once better known for housing the stonecutter artisans guild that renovated the orphanage, but it is now renowned for this unique tapestry conservation center.

Much of the studio's work is commissioned by the cathedral, which owns an impressive number of textiles, including two collections that date to the seventeenth century. Major museums, such as the Metropolitan Museum of Art and the Frick Collection, as well as private collectors, also rely on the center's expertise. The conservators' approach is minimal, meaning that they hope to do the least-invasive work possible in order to maintain the integrity of the textile, whether needlepoint, tapestry, upholstery, or even a costume. They first thoroughly analyze each piece, noting its background and subject matter. Depending on the fibers, the conservators then clean the piece, either wet or dry, with suction or spot cleaning. Next, they add yarn or fabric to worn areas with custom dyes that are mixed in an adjacent room using old recipes.

The large, bright studio offers direct access to the cathedral. It is sparsely populated with six women at work on both incredibly large looms and on minuscule pieces, surrounded by various needles, thimbles, and threads. Some mend holes while others back tapestries, and together, they try to understand the structure of a given piece and how to match or reproduce that structure in an affected area. When a piece is complete, the women hang it from the ceiling, or as high as needed, so they can take a step back and gaze upon it, ensuring their work has been done properly. The conservation center also offers an apprenticeship program to train the next generation.

Taxidermist

dlife Preservations

Lackawanna Avenue, Unit 104
odland Park, NJ 07424
890 1516
w.wildlifepreservations.com

Since prehistoric times, humans have been adapting the hides and skins of animals for clothing and shelter. As the methods of hunting improved over the millennia, so did techniques of preserving the animal skins and hides. In the 1800s, hunters began to glorify their prey by filling the skins with rags and cotton fibers for display. This crude image looms over the taxidermy industry, and bears little resemblance to the modern practice.

In the early twentieth century, taxidermy became an art form in the hands of Carl E. Akeley, William T. Horneday, Coleman Jonas, and Leon Pray, who developed anatomically correct mannequins. They were able to capture every tendon, muscle, and ligature to uncannily realistic results, and position their finished products in appropriate, lifelike settings.

George A. Dante Jr.'s passion for taxidermy was sparked at the tender age of seven after reading a book about animals. He started frequently visiting New York's American Museum of Natural History, where he carefully studied the animals on display: their positions, habitats, and even their meals. He pursued a degree in art at the School of Visual Arts in New York, where he completed his first taxidermy models, starting a small studio in his parents' basement. Once he was able to support himself, he moved his studio to its current location.

Each new project begins with a phone call from a client who describes the animal's measurements. The skin arrives from the tannery salted or frozen, and Dante begins to work on it immediately. Each animal provides its unique challenges so each form must be custom made. The most difficult work is never actually seen—it's done on the inside, with clay and wire to mimic the animal's inner workings. It takes Dante about two weeks to complete the skin's fitting and to capture the subject's facial expressions.

Finishing aquatic life presents unique challenges. When a frozen fish arrives, Dante creates a mold of it, casts it in sand made of fiberglass, and then paints it. The tricky part is capturing the fish's transparency. Dante fashions its habitat and surroundings from plastic as well as dried flowers, driftwood, ferns, and rocks, which he stores in containers that line the warehouse. For many of his projects, he seeks the advice of museums and scientists to determine the habitat of a particular species, sometimes an endangered or extinct one.

Atelier du Jour
West 37th Street
New York, NY 10018
478 7549
w.latelierdujour.com

Pascale Ouattara's studio in Manhattan's Fashion District is decorated with travel souvenirs, ranging from tchotchkes discovered in nearby flea markets to scraps of handmade Peruvian fabric from South America. Its walls are filled with samples of her embroidery as well as her own paintings. The centerpiece of the space is an oversize table where she realizes her projects.

Ouattara, a tall woman with an inviting smile, studied painting at the École des Beaux-Arts in Paris. Since she was a child, her Elna sewing machine has been at her side. After school, she worked for a costume design store in New York, and eventually opened her own atelier. She now caters to interior designers and private clients, most of whom come armed with inspiration, such as a piece of fabric that she imbues with life. She can create almost anything, from a pillow with antique embroidery, to a tent, to a fabric horse saddle. Everything leaves the studio with couturelike finishes.

Lately, she has been collaborating on location with set designers, although she equally enjoys working on residential interior projects. She recently finished a pouf crocheted in Liberty of London fabric, a tent for a movie set, and pillows for an antique textile collector. Ouattara simply delights in experimenting with fabrics, and even enjoys the freedom of embellishing textiles that many others would consider already "finished."

Upholsterer

elier de France
1 Van Brunt Street
1 Floor, Suite 11D
ooklyn, NY 11231
3 643 2288
w.atelierdefrance.com

Bruno Lopez is a walking encyclopedia of historical upholstery. He studied at the École Faidherbe in France, after which he became the upholsterer in residence at the Hôtel Ritz, Paris. By 1982, he was ready to pursue another passion, and he moved to Boston to attend the Berklee College of Music. By the time his son was born in 1986, he already wanted to return to his original trade.

He opened a shop in Massachusetts, although he relocated to Brooklyn, New York, shortly thereafter. Today, his large atelier is open and airy, with a view of the Gowanus Canal and New York Harbor.

Museums, conservators, and restorers seek out his unique skills. Many of his pieces are still made to measure: he works from a drawing to make and adjust the product by hand. Sometimes, he lets visitors observe the stitching (feather stitches, straight stitches) and knotting, which is done in linen and flax thread, or nylon, depending on the fabric and the finished product's intended use. He has found tools in the United States, but still relies on European sources for most of his materials, such as high-quality burlap. He enjoys new commissions, and works with clients to create dream furniture.

For Lopez, fashioning a successful piece involves understanding its shape, style, and volume, and staying historically true to its original form. He plans to take pictures of each step of the process as documentation for future generations of artisans.

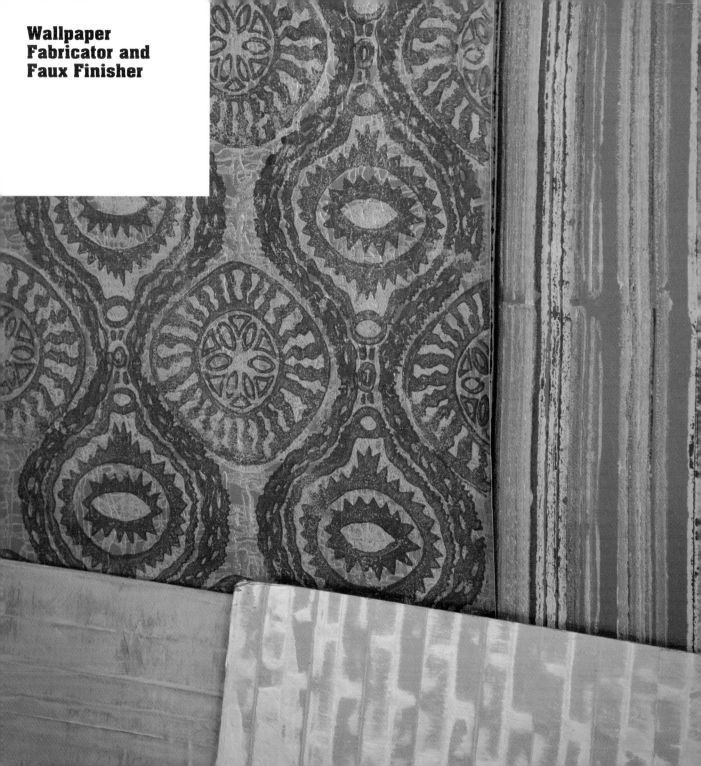

e Alpha Workshops
West 29th Street
w York, NY 10001
594 7320
w.alphaworkshops.org

In 1995, Kenneth Wampler, an energetic man with a theater and design background, opened a decorative painting studio with a mission to train and provide jobs for New Yorkers with AIDS and HIV. Today, Alpha Workshops employs many artists, all of whom undergo rigorous decorative-painting and faux-finishing training. The studio takes up four floors in a Chelsea loft building, with doors leading to studios for furniture painting, lamp making, and wallpaper making. Even though it's located in the middle of Manhattan, Alpha Workshops takes a cue from the hand-painting traditions of an Italian Renaissance studio.

Alpha artisans started out creating hand-painted wall coverings; today, they can create almost anything on commission, making them a favorite source for renowned interior designers such as Jamie Drake. Most of these jobs are on site, and involve glazing walls, gilding ceilings, or faux-finishing woodwork. Every year, Alpha artisans produce new collections of accessories, furniture, and lamps; some of their most popular patterns have also been printed as a collection for Thibault wall-coverings. They also have a textile collection with Pollack and a vinyl wall-covering collection with Koroseal. A collection of rugs with Edward Fields is forthcoming.

Students attend Alpha Workshops to learn the skills for each application, eventually joining the studio full time, depending on their interests and talents in the different stages and processes, such as casting, painting, and on-site installations. In the lamp department, lamps are designed, cast, gilded, painted, and wired. One particularly popular model, Eden Roc—homage to the famous Miami hotel—is a floor lamp with a chunky gilt base. Once the lamp has been cast in a mold, it must be heavily sanded before silver and gold leaf can be applied. In another department, artisans make tiles from polymer clay. They roll and cut the clay, create interesting patterns, fire and glaze the piece, and yield playful, unique tiles.

The largest part of the studio is the cheerful, paint-splattered wallpaper department. The papers are still completely handmade, which allows for flexibility and endless experimentation with patterns, effects, and color combinations. One artisan makes a stencil and another makes a block print, while someone else plays with folding a sheet of paper to create a new effect. Across the room, someone concocts paints to find a new consistency.

Weaver

Thistle Hill Weavers
1 Chestnut Ridge Road
Cherry Valley, NY 13320
3 284 2729
ww.thistlehillweavers.com

Rabbit Goody is a self-described hippie trained as a textile historian. She traveled to Lyon, France, to learn how to use antique looms. She started to spin, then moved on to vertical weaving; eventually, she took over the loom at Prelle, a French weaving institution. Armed with this knowledge and experience, she opened an atelier in Cherry Valley, New York, in a space that looks like a warehouse next to a junkyard, filled with antique looms dating from the 1890s to the 1960s. The inside of her studio resembles a museum, but with working looms—artful machines making beautiful music. The advantages of old looms are both their accuracy and the authenticity they lend to the finished product.

Five weavers work together, doing a bit of everything at Thistle Hill. They have not formally apprenticed under another weaver, but rather have developed an understanding that has deepened through time and on-the-job experience with the process and the material. Thistle Hill weaves—whether for carpets, clothing, or upholstery, or for individuals or interior designers—are fixtures in blockbuster films and period television shows, such as *John Adams*, *Shutter Island*, *The Curious Case of Benjamin Button*, and *No Country for Old Men*. Depending on the story line, two coats, for instance, may be needed for a single role: each one must look new when a character first wears it, and then appear to be aged for the character later in life.

Almost all of the yarn woven at Thistle Hill is organically dyed cotton and silk. All of the looms come from old mills, and were manufactured mostly in the South. Each loom is labeled with its name, provenance, and weave specialty. Rabbit believes the older the loom, the nicer the feel of the finished product.

Weaving is a slow process that involves securing the right tension on the loom, producing a small woven sample for a client, and then reproducing the same result in final, actual scale. And even after the weave appears to be complete, it's not yet finished. The fabric must be washed to achieve the right finish and definition, which sometimes makes it look as old as the looms themselves.

Wood Turner

Decrescenzo
9 Route 212
gerties, NY 12477
246 9301

From an early age, Jim Decrescenzo fiddled with wood, first learning basic carpentry and then slowly mastering the more demanding skills needed for wood turning. At age twenty-three, he committed to the practice, building his own lathes, and creating bigger and bigger, more serious pieces, while he attended seminars at Cooper Union in an attempt to perfect his craft. In the years since, he has done work for numerous furniture designers across the country. He prefers oversize pieces, and has established his own following among collectors and wood connoisseurs. He now lives in Saugerties, New York, where his home and studio blend into one, with notes and sketches covering most surfaces. He is unstoppable, and can transform the most monstrous piece of wood into any imaginable shape.

As with most art forms, wood turning requires tremendous concentration. Decrescenzo works barefoot—he loves the feel of wood chips beneath his feet—and wears extremely thick gloves and protective glasses. Precision is key, and he seems always to be taking measurements and creating patterns. Tools, especially sharp ones, are critical to a wood turner, and many of Decrescenzo's are handmade, such as his lathe, which enables him to turn large logs into a fantastic assortment of shapes.

The techniques involved in wood turning have not changed since the 1919 advent of the Milton and Wohlers Woodturning Course. However, for Decrescenzo, each day yields a new challenge. Because of their consistent density, walnut and cherry are his favorite woods; other species offer their own advantages, such as the delightful surprise of uncovering a knot after working on trunk for a few hours.

Index of Artisans

Architectural Hardware Maker
E. R. Butler & Co.
55 Prince Street
New York, NY 10012
212 925 3565
www.erbutler.com

Art Conservator
Simon Parkes
502 East 74th Street
New York, NY 10021
212 734 3920

Basket Weaver
Jonathan Kline
5126 Mott Evans Road
Trumansburg, NY 14886
607 387 5718
www.blackashbaskets.com

Bicycle Builder
Coast Cycles
50 Troutman Street
Brooklyn, NY 11206
646 724 1596
www.johnnycoast.com

Billiards Maker
Blatt Billiards
809 Broadway
New York, NY 10003
212 674 8855
www.blattbilliards.com

Bookbinder
Paper Dragon Books
330 Morgan Avenue, Suite 301
Brooklyn, NY 11211
718 782 8100
www.paperdragonbooks.com

Calligrapher
Bernard Maisner
165 West 66th Street, Suite 8K
New York, NY 10023
212 477 6776
www.bernardmaisner.com

Carpenter
Miya Shoji
145 West 26th Street
New York, NY 10001
212 243 6774
www.miyashoji.com

Car Restorer
Northumberland Engineering
118 Mariner Drive
Southampton, NY 11968
631 287 2213
www.northumberlandenterprises
.com

Ceramicist
Inma Barrero
429 East 77th Street
New York, NY 10028
646 221 1814

Decoupage Artist
John Derian Company
6 East 2nd Street
New York, NY 10003
212 677 3917
www.johnderian.com

Decoy Carver
Robert Hand
203 Madison Street
Sag Harbor, NY 11963
631 725 2314

Embroiderer
Penn & Fletcher
21-07 41st Avenue, 5th Floor
Long Island City, NY 11101
212 239 6868
www.pennandfletcher.com

Floral Designer
L'Olivier Floral Atelier
19 East 76th Street
New York, NY 10021
212 774 7676
213 West 14th Street
New York, NY 10011
212 255 2828
www.lolivier.com

Framer
Eli Wilner & Company
1525 York Avenue
New York, NY 10028
212 744 6521
www.eliwilner.com

Furniture Conservator
Fine Wood Conservation, Ltd.
481 Van Brunt Street
Brooklyn, NY 11231
718 802 1659
www.woodconservation.com

Furniture Maker
Chris Lehrecke
415 Warren Street
Hudson, NY 12534
845 802 6187
www.chrislehrecke.com

Glassblower
Michiko Sakano Glass
232 3rd Street, Suite E001
Brooklyn, NY 11215
917 783 0893
www.michikosakano.com

Glass Engraver
Tomas Tisch Studio
499 Van Brunt Street, Suite 10B
Brooklyn, NY 11231
718 643 9028
www.tomastisch.org

Glover
Daniel Storto
40 North Main Street
Gloversville, NY 12078
518 725 4803
www.danielstorto.com

Hatter
Rod Keenan
202 West 122nd Street
New York, NY 10027
212 678 9275
www.rodkeenannewyork.com

Hooked Rug Weaver
Stephen T. Anderson
2417 3rd Avenue
Bronx, NY 10451
212 319 0815
www.stephentanderson.com

Illuminator and Calligrapher
The Gorst Studio
210 Harrison Avenue
Harrison, NY 10528
914 815 0996
www.gorststudio.com

Lacquerer
Nancy Lorenz
315 West 36th Street
New York, NY 10018
212 989 1354
www.nancy-lorenz.com

Letterpress Printer
Swayspace
232 Third Street, Studio E104
Brooklyn, NY 11215
718 596 3520
www.swayspace.com

Lighting Fitter
Rambusch Lighting
160 Cornelison Avenue
Jersey City, NJ 07302
201 333 2525
www.rambusch.com

Luthier
Nathaniel Rowan
232 3rd Street, Studio E101
Brooklyn, NY 11215
natrowan@earthlink.net

Mannequin Maker
Ralph Pucci
44 West 18th Street
New York, NY 10011
212 633 0452
www.ralphpucci.net

talsmith
s Métalliers Champenois
2nd Avenue
:erson, NJ 07514
8 279 3573
vw.l-m-c.com

saicist
egory Muller Associates
5 Kent Avenue
ooklyn, NY 11211
8 599 6220
vw.gregorymullerassoc.com

on Fabricator
e Brite Neon
2 3rd Street
ooklyn, NY 11215
8 855 6082
vw.litebriteneon.com

permaker
eu Donné
5 West 36th Street
w York, NY 10018
2 226 0573
vw.dieudonne.org

no Maker
einway & Sons
teinway Place
ng Island City, NY 11105
8 721 2600
vw.steinway.com

eater
rry's Pleating & Stitch
7 West 38th Street, Room 314
w York, NY 10018
2 268 1378

ilter
ie Floersch
5 West 36th Street, Suite 11C
w York, NY 10018
6 338 3272
vw.juliefloersch.com

Sculptural Metalsmith
Kammetal
60 Seabring Street
Brooklyn, NY 11231
718 722 7400
www.kammetal.com

Shipwright
CH Marine Yachts
68 Cartwright Road
Shelter Island, NY 11964
800 584 2231
www.chmarineyachts.com

Silversmith
Valentin Yotkov
68 Jay Street, Suite 210
Brooklyn, NY 11201
718 852 8640
www.valentinyotkov.com

Stained Glass Restorer
Venturella Studio
32 Union Square East, Suite 1110
New York, NY 10003
212 228 4252
www.venturellastudio.com

Stonemason
A. Ottavino Corporation
80-60 Pitkin Avenue
Ozone Park, NY 11417
718 848 9404
www.ottavinostone.com

Straw Marqueter
Sandrine Viollet
505 Driggs Avenue
Brooklyn, NY 11211
718 782 1727
www.atelierviollet.com

Tableware Maker
Sydney Albertini
519 Acabonac Road
East Hampton, NY 11937
631 907 9371
www.sydneysalbertini.com

Tanner
Pergamena
11 Factory Street
Montgomery, NY 12549
845 649 5806
www.pergamena.net

Tapestry Conservator
Textile Conservation Laboratory
The Cathedral of St. John
the Divine
1047 Amsterdam Avenue
New York, NY 10025
212 316 7523
www.stjohndivine.org

Taxidermist
Wildlife Preservations
192 Lackawanna Avenue, Unit 104
Woodland Park, NJ 07424
973 890 1516
www.wildlifepreservations.com

Textile Designer
L'Atelier du Jour
325 West 37th Street
New York, NY 10018
917 478 7549
www.latelierdujour.com

Upholsterer
Atelier de France
481 Van Brunt Street, 4th Floor
Suite 11D
Brooklyn, NY 11231
718 643 2288
www.atelierdefrance.com

**Wallpaper Fabricator
and Faux Finisher**
The Alpha Workshops
245 West 29th Street
New York, NY 10001
212 594 7320
www.alphaworkshops.org

Weaver
Thistle Hill Weavers
101 Chestnut Ridge Road
Cherry Valley, NY 13320
518 284 2729
www.thistlehillweavers.com

Wood Turner
Jim Decrescenzo
1439 Route 212
Saugerties, NY 12477
845 246 9301

About the Author

Nathalie Sann is the author of three books and is a master artisan herself, specializing in embroidery and gold leaf. Her work has been featured in *Marie Claire*, *Elle*, *House & Garden*, *House Beautiful*, and *Town & Country*.

About the Photographer

Ted Sann is responsible for all the photographs in this book. Sann created many award-winning campaigns during a thirty-year career at BBDO Advertising, where he was chief creative officer.